QUICKBOOKS

*A Beginner's Guide to Bookkeeping and
Accounting for Small Businesses*

By Michael Kane

Table of contents

INTRODUCTION

Owning a business requires certain financial obligations. Your main goal is to make money to keep the business running, pay for goods, expenses, employees and yourself. You have state and federal responsibilities too, such as federal and state taxes, employment taxes, sale taxes and incorporation fees (depending on the size and type of business).

Your obligations tell you to keep as much money in the business as possible, while meeting your financial responsibilities. Spending too much on expenses, such as occasional business needs, can decrease the amount of money you have for the more important expenses and bills.

Hiring an accountant who is a bookkeeper and accountant is one choice. The person fulfills the main functions for the financial responsibilities your company has. You can decide to have a bookkeeper that comes in once a week to take care of the daily, weekly, and monthly tasks, and have an accountant for the tax liabilities. For example, the accountant would file the yearly tax data and create the W-2 forms for employee tax information.

A third choice is for you to be the bookkeeper or have a staff member do part-time bookkeeping responsibilities and have an accountant to call for the important business financial questions and obligations.

If you plan on doing most of the bookkeeping in-house, whether someone comes in once a week or a staff member you already have takes care of the little things, then using accounting software, with bookkeeping capabilities is the perfect solution.

Prior to the 1980s, most bookkeeping was done by hand, using ledgers, notebooks and other manual concepts. With the invention of a more affordable computer, word processor concepts where you could create spreadsheets became the norm. One company decided to go further and create a program that would handle bookkeeping tasks and be useful for accountants. The company, Intuit, is behind QuickBooks and is the topic of discussion.

QuickBooks can be added when you start a business, to an existing business, or when you decide to switch from a different accounting and bookkeeping software. You might have used Quicken, Money, or something else that exists, so learning how to use QuickBooks and who it is meant for is going to help you decide if you want to use the program.

You are going to learn:

1. What QuickBooks is.
2. How it works.
3. Why you want to use it.
4. Its affordability.
5. The various tasks it helps with.

As you continue through the guide, you will gain:

- Step by step instructions.

- Knowledge for how to perform an every day task up to occasional duties.
- Tips for quick usability.

By the end, you will understand whether you want to buy or download the program, use it online, and how much time and money it is going to save you. You are also going to know if switching to QuickBooks or adding it new is the right method for your company. You have a lot of decisions to make, including how you want to learn to use the program. Thank you for choosing this comprehensive guide to business and the implementation of QuickBooks.

CHAPTER 1

QUICKBOOKS, ACCOUNTING AND BOOKKEEPING

Starting a business or taking over an older business that may not be up on its technology will require you to understand the various tools you can use to help you successfully run your company. QuickBooks is one way you can perform bookkeeping and accounting duties when running a business.

What is QuickBooks?

QuickBooks is a business software for the financial responsibilities your company has. You can do bookkeeping and accounting with QuickBooks software. Some businesses use the software only for paying their employees, while others use the full repertoire available.

QuickBooks is designed mostly for the small business retailer, contractor, manufacturer or distributor. It is also helpful for attorneys, non-profits and CPAs. The businesses that get the most use out of QuickBooks have under 50 employees, with less than $20 million in revenue.

History of QuickBooks

In 1494, Luca Pacioli invented a double-entry bookkeeping concept, which became known throughout the world. Pacioli was not the first to have bookkeeping and accounting practices. However, he was the first to describe the debits and credits concept. Pacioli used debits and credits in journals and ledgers, which we still have today. By 1887, accounting became a profession with the first CPAs licensed in 1896. Large firms started adding accountants on retainer, having accountants audit the books for performance and other reasons. Eventually, we hit a point where technology became useful beyond what Pacioli and early accountants could have imagined.

QuickBooks is part of Intuit's software line, founded in 1983 by Scott Cook and Tom Proulx. The first program they created was called Quicken. Quicken is still around today. While some functions are similar to QuickBooks, it is also meant for larger businesses. In 1992, they launched QuickBooks, which has become the most popular accounting software a small company can have. At the outset, QuickBooks had some limiting factors in what it could do and was unable to work with complex businesses. Many small businesses found tracking vendors, writing checks, paying employees and keeping up with accounts payable and receivable was doable with the software package. In 2001, QuickBooks gained new updates that made it worthwhile and, in 2015, it became the most used accounting software for small businesses.

QuickBooks has evolved from the 1992 version. At first, you had to buy the program and install it on your computer. It came in a box, with a manual and a disc. It is available in this way today, although the manual is now online. In the new millennium, QuickBooks, like many software companies, started offering the program via download from their website. It has evolved even further to be a program you access without downloading to your computer. The plans and pricings discussed later explain the CD-ROM option, download from the net, and online usage.

Intuit never stops trying to improve their accounting software. They offer continual updates and add new features that their clients will find useful.

Difference between Bookkeeping and Accounting

Bookkeeping is the recording of financial transactions. A bookkeeper is a person who enters in the data, maintains the current information, creates reports if necessary, but overall makes sure everything is recorded. Accounting is where the interpretation, classification, analysis, reporting and summation of financial data occurs. Accountants take the records created by the bookkeeper to create cash flow, taxes, employee paychecks and help show the financial health of the company through the analysis of the reports.

For a business to succeed bookkeeping and accounting must be done. How you set this up will determine the amount paid out for services, versus what you keep in-house. The size of your company also weighs in on the choice you make to have an accountant prepare documents or whether you prepare everything yourself. You are never going to be an accountant doing your taxes as a business, even if you have QuickBooks, but you can create as much data and reports as possible and handle small accounting concepts, without paying a large sum to an accountant.

Many small businesses have an accountant to do the taxes and create the W-2 forms for employee tax season. Otherwise, the owners take care of making payments, creating reports, interpreting the data for the next year projections, and other financial requirements.

Accountants work on an hourly basis, many charging over $100 per hour for their services. Imagine if you have an accountant who creates the paychecks on a bi-monthly timeframe, pays the sales tax, and employee taxes. Let's say it takes an hour for each task, so you pay out $400 per month. What if you could save that money, and only pay out $100 each month?

Why is Accounting Software Essential?

Accounting software is essential for a multitude of reasons the least of which is ensuring your company has proper accounting records for tax season. Accounting software can streamline your financial process to ensure you are tracking the success of your business, paying companies and employees on time, and providing a clear picture of your business' financial health. It is possible to not have an accounting software in-house, if you have hired an accountant. However, you can save yourself a lot of time and expense by having accounting software at the company to record everything.

The benefits of accounting software include:

- Accuracy – you can reduce human error in calculations.
- Speed – using software helps you become faster at the financial data you require.
- Cost – the software is often less expensive than hiring an accountant to do much of your financial work. Remember the example of $100 versus $400 per month?
- Reports – nearly all cash flow reports you might need, including what vendors have not been paid or accounts have not paid, can be tracked.
- Tax – taxes not only for employees, but also for your business can be calculated using the software. You can use the software to complete your income taxes with less spent on an accountant.

Excel Spreadsheet vs. Accounting Software

Old-school methods from when computers were just starting to be used, include using an excel spreadsheet to generate reports, keep track of employee payments, and more. While it might work when you have a couple of employees, a few vendors, or just sell services, it is much easier to use accounting software. Excel spreadsheets require you to lock certain columns, understand how Excel works, and create your own formulas.

For example, you would need to keep a ledger of incoming and outgoing funds. You would also need:

- A template for employee hours, taxes, net, and gross earnings to calculate your tax liability and create paychecks.
- A template for vendors.
- A vendor file with address, returns information, and contact information.

The list can go on. You would need to manually create all these things, save them in proper folders, and find them again when you need to work with the Excel sheets you create. It takes time. It takes effort. It is more work than using accounting software that keeps everything tidy.

Accounting software, like QuickBooks, does everything for you without the time and thought process spent on creating what you need.

As you buy a business or start a company, you need to ask yourself if you want to work smarter or harder. Tools that take less time to perform necessary actions ensure you are working smarter. With QuickBooks you have more time to work on bringing money in than bookkeeping and accounting concepts.

CHAPTER 2

WHY DO BUSINESSES USE QUICKBOOKS?

QuickBooks is not the only accounting and bookkeeping software on the market. However, small businesses have discovered it has numerous benefits beyond other software options. It is designed for small companies who often do not have the funds to hire a bookkeeper and accountant. QuickBooks is also easier to learn and integrate into a business than other software programs out there. While this last fact is an opinion, having used Quicken and QuickBooks, there are simple features in QuickBooks that are more complicated in Quicken. How the program works, how easy it monitors cash flow, customer support from QuickBooks, and the training provided by the company all make QuickBooks worth using.

How It Works

QuickBooks allows you to perform business tasks relating to bookkeeping and accounting. Some of the tasks you need to do occur daily, while others are less frequent. The program takes the information you provide regarding revenue and expenses, allocates information to certain customers and vendors, while keeping track of the bills that are outgoing and in-coming. From the information supplied, QuickBooks maintains your bank account balances to show you how much money you have in the bank, and what needs to be spent. You can also draft reports to overview the financial health of your company. The following information breaks down the three parts to help your understanding of how QuickBooks works for businesses.

You can break QuickBooks into three parts:

- Daily Tasks
- Occasional Tasks
- Housekeeping Procedures

Daily Tasks

Daily tasks are the everyday items you take care of for bookkeeping.

- Creating Invoices
- Creating Credit Memos
- Payments
- Paying Bills
- Inventory
- Checkbook Details
- Paying Electronically

Each business has a need to create invoices. Invoices are sent out to those with accounts, such as a library picking up books on account, at a bookstore, and then paying their bill.

Businesses also send out credit memos when an overpayment or issue has occurred.

For payments, you typically send out invoices, but sometimes you need to keep on top of the company to ensure you get paid. You can also use QuickBooks as a Point of Sale system depending on your company's goods and services. You can use it to take payments for services or goods.

QuickBooks keeps track of the bills you pay and the bills that are becoming due. When you get an invoice or packing slip from a company for goods you bring in, QuickBooks can keep track of the payment terms and alert you to a payment needing to be made, as well as keep track in your check register of the payments you have made.

Furthermore, if you have a company where you make payments online for goods or services, you can use QuickBooks to send payments or even to take payments using electronic means or credit cards.

Occasional Tasks

On occasion, your business will have things that need to be done like printing checks. You probably don't send out payments each day, so these tasks are more about the weekly or monthly options.

- Printing Checks

- Payroll
- Creating the Budget

Printing checks is often a thing you will do once a week, and then twice monthly for payroll. Creating a budget is also something you do once a quarter and a yearly basis, which means you need to know that you can use QuickBooks for these tasks and how it works.

Housekeeping

These are chores you do occasionally, most often for accounting needs and business health.

- Balancing the check register
- Reporting, such as sales tax and other taxes
- Job Estimating, Billing, and Tracking
- File Management
- Fixed Assets and Vehicle Lists

When you get your bank statement, you reconcile your check register with the information on the bank statement. You also have sales tax and other taxes to pay or report about monthly.

QuickBooks is available to help you estimate job expenses, employment needs, billing and tracking of those jobs.

As with any business, you need hard copies of the files and a way to manage the different vendors, suppliers, customers and sales. These are housekeeping concepts when it comes to making sure your files are up-to-date.

Fixed asset and vehicle list maintenance is something you do when a new asset is purchased, an old one is sold or disposed of, and when you add new vehicles or trade out old ones. Your company needs a list of the assets; particularly, for the valuation and depreciation of them.

These are just a few of the topics that help you understand how QuickBooks works to provide you the information you need to perform daily, monthly, and housekeeping business tasks.

Cash Flow Monitoring

QuickBooks is also designed to help you track the cash flow you have. In several ways, you can print reports to show how much money is coming in and how much is going out. You can create reports that show where the money is going. From the cash flow monitoring reports, you also get suggestions from online support or through your accountant. These suggestions help you improve or streamline your company, so you are handling the cash flow better.

Customer Support

QuickBooks is something you can learn on your own. You are reading a guide to help you with the basic information, such as how to set up payroll, but you also have Intuit support through phone and chat that helps train you for the various tasks you want to perform. Customer support is based on the level of QuickBooks plan you buy. Simple questions can be answered without a support plan. For those who want more, such as training classes, and hands-on computer help you may want to pick a QuickBooks plan that includes more hands-on customer support.

Training Classes

Not everyone can read a book and learn everything they need to know. Sometimes it also helps to have personal training to streamline the process and cut out the details you don't need to know when it comes to QuickBooks. The training classes provided can be live, self-paced, or through personal support chats.

For customer support concepts, more details are coming with regard to the level of support based on the fee you pay for the QuickBooks program. You also have different options when it comes to training employees who may use the software to help you in the office. As more topics surface, the information will be discussed. The idea is whether you are the owner of the company or the one doing bookkeeping/accounting tasks with QuickBooks, you can use the information here to help you.

CHAPTER 3

PICKING THE RIGHT QUICKBOOKS PLAN

There are two main ways you can add QuickBooks to your store:

1. Online
2. CD-ROM

It is important to choose the right choice for you with regard to your accounting needs. Some businesses want the CD versus an online version. The benefits they require are minor compared to the options with online plans and pricing.

CD-ROM Choices

For a one-time payment, you can purchase QuickBooks, either in CD-ROM form or downloaded from the online website. It installs on your desktop and is accessed without the need of an Internet connection. The cheapest version is QuickBooks Pro. It is designed to help you maximize tax deductions, organize expenses, track business performance, gain financial, sales and tax reports, and you do not need accounting knowledge to use it. It will not come with unlimited customer support. You can ask a few questions when you set it up, but mostly you will need to refer to books like this to help you get through the daily, occasional and housekeeping tasks.

The Pro Plus option provides everything the Pro version has and adds unlimited customer support, automated data back-up with recovery options and software upgrades. When a new company begins or is transitioning into the online world, you can also add on hosting services, which help you update your online information, keep in touch with your account, and you don't need to pay for servers or IT maintenance with the hosting add-on. The Pro Plus is an annual subscription.

Now, you can gain even more if you are willing to pay a high price. An annual subscription to Enterprise 19.0 offers software that one to thirty people can use, with six times the capacity of the other programs, increased tools for reporting, inventory, and pricing, plus access to the QuickBooks Priority Circle Program. The Enterprise version is a point of sale concept, which is why it has an annual subscription, even though you can buy it as a CD-ROM version.

Most software programs, even Microsoft Word are digital, where you download the file directly from Microsoft's website. The need for CD-ROMs is ending, but that is not going to change the fact that for the Pro version you can pay once and use the software for years.

The pricing can change. In fact, as the details were being researched on Intuit, the pricing showed a discount for the payment options. If you walk into an office store to buy software or go online, you will see similar pricing.

- Pro - $299.95 once
- Pro Plus - $299.95 annually
- Enterprise 19.0 - $1155 annually

Plans and Pricing

If you decide to go with an online plan, you will pay a monthly fee. The plans are as follows.

1. Freelancer: a plan for the self-employed, which is normally $10 per month. It allows you to track income and expenses, capture and organize receipts, estimate quarterly taxes, invoices and accept payments, run basic reports and track your vehicle miles.

2. Advanced: a plan for $150 per month. It does everything the freelancer plan will do, but adds maximizing your tax deductions, running advanced reports, sending estimates, tracking sales and sales tax, managing bills, and it can support up to 25 individual users. You also get to track time, project profitability, inventory, and manager freelancers. It has smart reporting, quick invoicing, custom permissions, and Premium Care with Priority Circle.

3. Plus: for $60 per month, you can do everything the self-employed option gives you, along with maximizing tax deductions, running advanced reports, sending estimates, managing bills, tracking sales tax and sales, time, project profitability, and inventory. You can also manage freelancers and have up to 5 users.

4. Essentials: you do not have added customer support with essentials, but it can do everything the Plus does, except only up to three users can use the program. It is $35 per month.

5. Simple Start: it is like the freelancer except it helps with tax deductions, sales, sales tax, and sending estimates all for $20 a month.

All the plans have customer support, receipt capture, and app integration. You can also add other services such as self-service payroll, full-service payroll, on the plus, essentials and simple start programs. The advanced program has payroll options within the product for sale. The freelancer choice does not have payroll and cannot be upgraded.

Pricing can change. Discounts may be available.

With the above plans and pricing, you can login to QuickBooks online or download it to the desktop. You can always upgrade your plan by paying the upgraded monthly fee. You are not under any contract. While miles are tracked with the Freelancer option, it is not fully integrated as a mileage tracking option. QuickBooks is hoping to add mileage tracking to their plans, with more features. If you use the mobile apps, you do not pay extra.

When you visit Intuit to add QuickBooks to your business, you can search by:

- QuickBooks Online – these are the above plans discussed.

- QuickBooks Self Employed – an added feature to the self-employed option is adding TurboTax to the bundle, where you gain options to pay your estimated taxes directly from QuickBooks, transfers to TurboTax, and federal/state returns each year. A secondary option with TurboTax bundle is to pay a little more and get help from a CPA.

- Online Advanced – the plus and advanced packages from above.

- Desktop for Mac – the download, using a one-time payment. It is not a plan, but the software.

- Desktop Pro – the software download discussed as CD-ROM options.

- Desktop Premier – software downloads with one time or annual subscriptions depending on the features you wish to have. It is more advanced in business features, including more for industry specific companies, creating sales orders, and setting product and service prices. You can buy the Premier, Premier Plus, or Enterprise versions.

- QuickBooks Point of Sale – designed as more than a bookkeeping and accounting system, the POS allows you to accept credit card payments, ring sales, track inventory, set up customer programs, sync with the accounting software from

QuickBooks, and work with Microsoft Surface Pro systems.

Size and Type of Business

The size and type of business you are running will determine which QuickBooks program will work best for you. QuickBooks is designed for many types of businesses, but it tends to work with certain industries better such as contractors, attorneys, and manufacturers. For a point of sale system, it is very broad and not set up for some of the industry specific choices like selling books in a bookstore. It is more for retail such as clothing.

The size of your business matters because these programs are set up for under 50 users. Typically, a small business needs the program on their main computer for bookkeeping and accounting. However, if you have sales representatives selling your products, you may need to have access for all employees so they can look at the inventory and proceed with an order. You want to make sure that your QuickBooks plan supports the number of users you have or will potentially have soon.

For businesses, with a bookkeeper who comes in twice a week to manage payments, payroll, and other daily activities, buying the CD-ROM or downloading it for a one-time payment can be enough. It also gives you everything your accountant will require. When you need more support and features, it can be time to turn to the plans and pricings discussed where you pay a monthly fee. There is one reason to pay for the downloaded version and save it to your hard drive, versus logging in each month to an online program.

If your Internet is interrupted, you can still work with QuickBooks, where you cannot if you only have online access.

Now you have an understanding that the plans, pricing, and options for adding QuickBooks to your company are diverse. It is up to you to research further details based on your company needs, speak with customer service about the product that is right for you, and get started.

CHAPTER 4

TRAINING AND CUSTOMER SUPPORT

Intuit provides an "Intuit QuickBooks Community" and blog section for general customer support. It is available online. You also have "help" offline in the CD-ROM or download versions. Beyond Intuit, there are training courses provided by companies who partner with Intuit. These companies offer classes with certification. There are live training classes where you can go to a two-day seminar to learn how to use QuickBooks. You also have the webinar study for self-paced learning. We will examine the different options to help you decide the level of customer support you want from Intuit and whether you wish to also include training classes.

In-House Customer Support

If you find you are not getting answers from the "help" section in the downloaded version or you have the online version, you can go to the QuickBooks Community, and launch the support articles. The topics include:

- Getting Started
- Banking and Bank Feeds
- Account Management
- Reports and Accounting
- Income and Expenses
- Payments
- Employees and Payroll Taxes
- Inventory and Projects
- Apps
- Help Articles

You also have access to the blog. The blog offers timely articles that may not fit your needs. For example, one topic was about foreign currency transfers, and another was 8 free tax resources for small businesses. If you don't accept foreign currency, then it may not be of use to you. However, most companies want to save on tax resources, so there is something useful.

Online at QuickBooks, you can also launch the QuickBooks Tutorials section. It is broken into two departments, Small Business and Accountants. For the business user, the following are videos you can watch:

- What are QuickBooks Apps?
- Reconcile Your Accounts
- Add a User
- Export Company File to QuickBooks

- Online Banking Overview

Please note, there are dozens of videos. They are broken into topics from general accounting to invoicing, sales, taxes, and more.

Additional resources include Webinars, Resource Center and Support. The resource center offers guides, tools, and articles on starting and running a successful business. QuickBooks support provides help with any topic and any QuickBooks product.

The accounting tab also provides several videos and tutorials you may find useful, even if you are not an accountant. Such topics include introduction to QuickBooks online Self-Employed, using the accounting toolbox, using trial balance and more.

If you pay for it, you can call QuickBooks or start a live chat with a professional. You would click the live chat option while logged in to your QuickBooks program. If you are trying to order products or set up two or more bank accounts with QuickBooks, you can ask live chat questions and get it set up, without paying extra. It is after the setup and more in-depth questions you may have that require paying for the customer support services. But, remember you have books and online video guides to walk you through almost anything you might need to know.

Live Classes and Self-Paced Training

Intuit partners with at least one company. They endorse the training provided in a two-day live class in most large cities. The training is comprehensive. You are in a classroom setting, you get your questions answered, and you gain tips and tricks to help you work with the program. The training is set up as desktop or online training, where you go to a classroom with your computer.

You can also sign in via webinar, if there is not a class in your local area. If you want to take the training to the next level, you can go to the class, prepare for an exam, and then take an exam at a land-based location. The certification is great for anyone's resume.

Self-paced training is available for those who want to train around their busy schedule, gain the same knowledge as the two-day course, and use the training as they work. There are several self-paced options designed for various business people, running diverse types of businesses.

For anyone who wants to make an upgrade in their business skills for the company they work for or to increase their hiring desirability, the training courses plus certification are worthwhile. If you just want to have someone walk you through how to use the program, then going to the class or going with a self-paced option is the way to learn what you need and get your questions answered.

Now that you understand the features available to you via QuickBooks support, it is time to go back to the plans and pricing and decide whether you want to add customer support options, go with a training program, or muddle through on your own. Remember, most of the online, monthly payment options have full customer support as part of the package, and thus may be worth the extra cost,

QUICKBOOKS

plus the added features you gain over the one-time fee for the download version.

CHAPTER 5

SETTING UP QUICKBOOKS

QuickBooks is a simple install on your computer, if you decided to go with the desktop version. If you are using the online product, you won't need to install anything. However, you are going to set up the program with your business details, register your copy of QuickBooks, and start entering data, no matter the program choice you made.

QuickBooks Set Up for a New Business

Individuals who have a new business and use QuickBooks from the start have an easier time with the set up. There are fewer things to input at the beginning. You are working on the details such as vendors, suppliers, distributors, employees, and probably have one bank account for the business. Business owners who download the program after running their company for years have to "switch" over to QuickBooks, entering current data, but also everything that is relevant. It is the same if someone buys the business and will keep many of the vendors, employees, and other business concepts the business already has and adds QuickBooks.

QUICKBOOKS

QuickBooks will walk you through the set up. There are prompts for when and what information to enter. The basic steps are below and may change based on the version you are using.

1. Create a Username and Password (required at time of purchase or when you install the desktop version)

2. Set up company information (business name, address, email, website, Tax ID).

3. On the right side of the screen, go to your company name and click on it. This opens the account information. It shows your company details and allows you to upload your company logo. It will show up on your invoices, and other official documents.

4. Save the changes.

5. Add contact information including company phone.

6. In the address area, you can show your shipping and billing address. If they are the same you can mark that in this area, so your bills indicate where a company or person should send payment. Save the changes.

You are ready to start using QuickBooks.

Business Set Up when Adding QuickBooks

If you decided you needed accounting software after your business has been running for years, the set up will vary slightly.

1. Check to make sure the latest QuickBooks version will run on your computer. Older computers, such as anything previous to Windows 7 operating system, are no longer supported with updates or with most software programs.

2. If you are using an online version, you need to make sure your web browser can support the online login requirements, again, older systems may not be supported by the browser.

3. Follow the "set up" steps for a new business ensuring to input company name, address, phone, email address, website, and Tax ID number.

QuickBooks works for billing, receiving, Point of Sale, and payroll. More information needs to be added to use the aspects of the program you are paying for, such as payroll.

Vendors Set Up

Setting up vendors in QuickBooks is essential for paying bills. You can pre-populate vendor information in QuickBooks and keep track of expenses by vendor. It helps you create reports to see who you are spending the most money with, which is important for business health.

You can set up vendors manually, use an Excel file, or CSV file. If you are not computer savvy, it is better to have a local computer technician or QuickBooks walk you through how to import with excel or a .CSV file. If you have 10 vendors or fewer than adding them manually is an acceptable option. Uploading a .CSV file is the quickest method when you have the information electronically available and the understanding for how to import. (Note: some companies may be so old-school that manual entry is the only option even for thirty plus vendors. It is time consuming but worth every minute).

1. Sign in to your account, via desktop or online.

2. Go to the "Vendors" tab on the left-hand side of your screen.

3. Click on "New Vendor" on the right side of the screen.

4. Enter company name

5. Enter address, it should be the billing address.

6. Enter email, phone, website

7. If you know it, enter the billing rate, terms, any opening balance you have.

8. Add the account number you have with the vendor and their Tax ID.

There is a place to add billing and shipping addresses for all vendors. For instance, if the billing address is different to an address you would use for returns, you can make this clear when you add a vendor.

Any company that is not a corporation requires a 1099 form. You will want to mark the "track payments for 1099" for any company you spend over $600 with to ensure you are fulfilling your tax requirements.

Save the Vendor if you have finished completing the fields. There is an option of uploading attachments for specific vendors. For example, if there is any paperwork for the company you want to keep, you can add an attached file.

Once you are done with the first vendor, save, close that vendor, and start adding a new one. You can always go back into the Vendor area, click on a company, and edit the information. You can mark vendors who are inactive but keep the records of the company should you wish to use them again.

Add all the vendors you currently work with and, when this is done, move on to a new category, such as Employees.

Setting Up Employees for Payroll

Before you can pay your employees using the Payroll function, you need to add them to your QuickBooks program. You also want to understand the tax information you need to set up or have an accountant on hand to help you. Further details about creating paychecks will come later; however, it needs to be mentioned that you can gain help with payroll by paying for an added QuickBooks payroll service. The reasons for using an added service are discussed later.

Find the Employees Section:

1. Click on "Employees" in the left side menu.

2. Click "Add" employee.

3. The first screen is personal information, including legal name, address, and phone.

4. You need to enter the frequency of payroll, such as full-time, regular, part-time, or other options.

5. You will also add information from the W-4 form regarding withholding.

6. If your state has an employment tax, you will need to set it up based on your state requirements.

7. Enter the birthdate and hire date of your employees.

Once you have the employee details added under all tabs, including the withholding information for the employee, you can add a new employee. Continue the process until all employees are entered. You also have an option of adding part-time employees who may be inactive. You can mark them as inactive or active, as their status changes.

The "Employee" area is just to set up specific withholding information for the employee. To use Payroll, you need to set up the Payroll Taxes in a separate area, where the Federal and State taxes are automatically calculated. If you do not know this information, you will need an accountant to help you set it up.

Entering Payroll Taxes

You can manually create Payroll each time you pay an employee. We will discuss this later. However, if you want to make life easy and avoid missing any tax payments for Payroll, you should opt-in for the Payroll option with QuickBooks. Depending on your plan, it may require an extra fee, or you may be able to set it up and start using it right away. This section is solely the steps to get the correct taxes entered for what you will need to pay and how to calculate the deductions for your employees.

First, when you enter withholding information under each employee, you are one step closer to getting the Payroll taxes set up. The following are steps you will go through once you get into the navigation center under "taxes." You will go into the Payroll Tax Center and begin filling in the information to ensure you are in compliance.

1. Enter your business information into the Payroll taxes setup.

2. Add your FEIN

3. Using 941 or 944 Form for taxes, open the form and provide the information.

4. Set up the Payment/Deposit schedule for federal tax payments.

5. Enter your bank account and routing numbers

6. Use your online USER ID and Password for your bank to make the payments.

You are now set up to use QuickBooks for Payroll.

Tying Your Bank Accounts to QuickBooks

There are a few reasons you might want to have your bank accounts tied to QuickBooks. The first is to ensure you make payments and keep records as accurate as possible. QuickBooks enables you to reconcile your bank statement by importing the information and checking it against what you have entered as you paid bills and employees. You can set up more than one business bank account, if necessary. You might have two accounts, such as one you pay bills with and one you pay employees with, which means you need to check the correct account is assigned to the payments being made as you do them. You want to have a bank account tied to QuickBooks for supplies, like ordering more checks.

Typically, you set up one account first and then request QuickBooks to help you set up the second account, when you are ordering checks for those accounts. However, you can set up as many accounts as you want by creating two or more check registers.

1. Go to Chart of Accounts.

2. Type Ctrl N on the keyboard to open a new window.

3. Click "Bank."

4. Follow the on-screen prompts to enter the bank related information, including routing number and bank account number.

5. Save.

When you set up your bank accounts for QuickBooks, you will need to enter a "starting" balance. This information is to tell the program how much money is in the bank account right now, so when you reconcile the bank account later, the numbers will match. If you need to, you can adjust the balance during the reconciliation process to indicate the correct details. You do not have to add every bank account you have, but if you are going to use them for business reasons or if you are going to reimburse your personal account for a business expense, it is best to tie everything you can together in QuickBooks. It is easier in the long run than adding things later. But, of course, you can always add more details later.

You have completed the set up for QuickBooks. It is time to move on to more in-depth areas of QuickBooks to ensure you are using everything available to you in the accounting software. The arrangement of topics is in keeping with daily, occasional, and housekeeping tasks.

CHAPTER 6

BASIC STEPS TO OPERATING QUICKBOOKS - PART 1

Your focus, if you are going to hire an accountant or have one, is to use QuickBooks for bookkeeping. You want to understand the basic operations and then graduate to more in-depth topics. You will want to understand bookkeeping such as recording revenue, expenses, accounts payable and accounts receivable. Your ultimate goal is to run a functioning business at a profit, which takes employees, reports, and understanding of the company's bottom line. The basic steps for using and operating QuickBooks will help you do the aforementioned concepts.

Bookkeeping in QuickBooks

Snail mail is still a thing although many companies are going "paperless" by sending invoices and credit memos through email. However, the "tax man" has not changed their requirements. Businesses are required to keep their business files, including all details about expenses, accounts payables, accounts receivables, and payroll, on hand for seven years. You still need hard copies, in the event a computer dies, the backups disappear, and any number of things happen. It also makes good sense to have a hard copy, plus electronic versions of everything.

The point being made—you are going to record everything from the mail or email that is business related to your company's health. Bookkeeping is all about the data, which needs to be in the computer and in your files.

The basic steps to operating QuickBooks are all about the daily tasks you want to perform. It begins by creating invoices that are going to help you bring in the revenue.

Creating Invoices

Part of your task if you sell goods or services is to invoice companies or customers. We are not going to discuss what your business might do but give you the tools to help you. If you do not create many invoices, then this section is of little importance to you. But it is also worth knowing it exists.

You have done the preliminary work by setting up the vendors and customers you have.

Know the type of invoice you are creating, including product, service or professional.

1. Go to Customers

2. Select Create Invoices

3. Select the Invoice form you need, such as professional, product, service, or credit memo.

4. Identify the person receiving the invoice from your "customer" list.

5. You can decide to assign a "class" which would track the income. Class is how you are categorizing the products or services you are invoicing for, which helps you keep track of your inventory or services rendered.

6. Enter a date for the invoice

7. Give the invoice a number to help you track it.

8. If necessary, you can adjust the "billing" and "shipping" addresses.

9. Depending on the size of your business, you may also assign Purchase Order (PO) numbers.

10. Specify the agreed upon payment terms, such as net 30 days.

11. Add in other details that may apply, including name of sale rep, shipping date, shipping method, and whether it is FOB (free on board).

12. Make sure you enter a line for each item you are selling to this customer.

13. Specify any specific information or items

14. You can add a customer message.

15. Enter the sales tax

16. Print the invoice for packing and your files.

17. Save the invoice by clicking on "Save" you can save and create a new invoice or save and close out of the invoices if you are done for the moment.

You have the option of going in and correcting errors you make on invoices. We will look at that information later in troubleshooting tips. What you want to get used to is following the prompts. The information being asked is self-explanatory and something you should be used to providing on an invoice if you have been in any management, bookkeeping, or business-ownership position before.

The difference is using QuickBooks instead of Excel or handwriting the information. It keeps your communications professional, supplies clear terms, and helps the company or customer receiving the goods check everything is in the box or boxes.

Invoices also help you know exactly what money is outstanding and needs to be paid. Back in the explanation for why you want to use accounting software, it was discussed that QuickBooks enables you to complete daily tasks such as entering information and occasional tasks like tracking down money you are owed and re-invoicing if necessary.

By using the basic functions of QuickBooks, you can check the incoming payments to determine if you received the money you should have based on the payment terms provided to your vendors or customers.

Accounts receivable is just one section of your company that needs daily input. Your accounts payable should be tracked to help you make your payments on time.

Credit Memos

Your customers may have items "on account" such as goods they have not paid for because the terms are net 30 days or more. There are also times when your customer may need to send items back. Perhaps, the item was faulty, so they are returning it. Let's look at sending items back. We will use a bookstore example. When you send hardcover books back to the publisher or distributor because the softcover of a book comes out, it can create a cycle of new books and credit memos.

Issuing a credit memo to your customer helps you record the revenue you make accurately against deductions made to accounts. You want to know you are getting the correct amount of money from the customer, so you must record credit memos as much as you create invoices and record payments.

From the Customer menu:

1. Choose "Create credit memo/refund.

2. Identify the customer.

3. Add a date, number, and confirm you have the correct customer details.

4. Add a reason for the memo.

5. Save and Close or you can create a new memo.

The process helps you allocate credits you are giving to a customer when you are in the payment information. It is two-fold. The first step is making sure you notify the customer they have received a credit on their account, and you will adjust the amount owed on your end. The second step is to help the customer and you keep track of the actual amount due based on the terms of the invoice and any credits they received before payment was due.

Recording Revenue

Paying the bills and sending out invoices to make sure you get paid is part of any business. Another part of basic accounting is to keep up with outstanding payments you need to receive. Each time a check or credit card payment is made for an invoice, you want to keep track of that money. Your software needs to know money is coming in to ensure you are balanced with your bank statement. Part of your bookkeeper's job, or yours, is to record the revenue. Recording the revenue or payments is part of the accounts receivable function of accounting. It is also part of the daily tasks you perform, whether you sell goods or services. You might not deposit the money each day; however, you do reconcile your sales for services or goods each night.

What are the types of revenue?

- Payment for goods or services sold.
- Credit card charges.
- Cash earned in the point of sale system.

If you are a retail store, you will have credit card and cash earnings to record. You may also invoice for products you ship. For example, if you run a bookstore, you might ship books to a client out of town, invoice them, and receive a check in the mail. You might also have a library buy books from you on account and then you receive payment for those books later.

A service business may invoice for their services, such as coming by to fix the plumbing and giving the client a week to pay for those services.

If you distribute goods, such as being a publisher who sells books to a retail location, you invoice the bookstores and record the payments they make against their account balance.

The steps to record revenue, when it is a direct sale, are simple:

1. Under "Customer" choose "Enter Sales Receipt."

2. Identify who sent the payment.

3. Specify the reason for the receipt.

4. Provide a date.

5. Record the check number for the payment.

6. Enter the payment method.

7. Describe what was sold.

8. Enter sales tax.

9. Print receipt.

10. Save the sales receipt.

This type of record of inventory is if you are selling a product directly to the customer and need a receipt while they are in the store. You also have the choice of recording customer payments against invoices.

Customer Payments

Use this choice if you are logging revenue paid from invoices. You already understand how an invoice is entered. Now, you want to make sure you have the payment recorded against the invoice. A few things can happen. The customer may decide to pay only a partial amount on the invoice. The customer may pay the full amount. The client may also forget to pay on time, which is when you would need to send a reminder invoice. You can always go into invoices and print a new document to mail, you can edit invoices too, as a way to reflect the past due information.

The steps below are designed for a full or partial payment.

1. Under "Customers"

2. Choose "Receive Payments"

3. Find the customer who paid.

4. Specify the date the payment was made (if payment was made that day, record the date, if you are going through a backlog of bookkeeping use the date on the check or payment form.)

5. Enter the amount being paid.

6. You can also go into the "Pmt," drop down menu to choose the type of method used for the payment, such as check, credit card, or cash.

7. Enter the check number, if there is one.

8. You have the option of adding a memo.

9. At this point, you can also apply outstanding "credit" to the account, such as a credit memo you have yet to allocate to the customer.

10. Find the invoices the customer is paying for, to allocate those to the account.

11. If necessary, you can adjust for early payment or discounts not shown on the invoice.

12. Click Done

13. Click to "Record" the payment information by selecting "save and new" or "save and close."

Notice there is a place to assign a credit memo should a company, client, or customer be due money for returned or faulty items. You have already learned how to create a credit memo, and step 9 showed you how to apply the credit memo when you are recording the revenue (payment) the client sent.

Keeping on Top of Revenue Flow

You are running a business. You need to have a good inflow of money to keep going. When your customers are late with payments, it makes it difficult to continue running your business. There are ways to keep on top of your clients to ensure the money flows in and cutting off customers when they are showing they are unable to keep up with the payments owed.

QuickBooks has invoice reminders for you and your customers. If you use the online version, you would follow this procedure.

1. Gear Icon

2. Settings

3. Company Settings

4. Sales

5. Reminders

6. You can customize the reminder.

7. To send the reminder, go to the money bar and click on "Overdue."

8. Go to the client.

9. Find the action column, and from the drop-down menu, choose to send a reminder, and how you want to send it.

10. You can also create a "batch" action to send each client reminders of overdue payments. Under the filter option on the left of the customer list, you can use the drop-down menu to select batch actions and choose an action to take.

You have the option of emailing, printing, or sharing invoice to send as a reminder.

In the online version, you will always see the money bar on the homepage. When you open it, you see open invoices, overdue, and payments made. You want to make certain you close an invoice as paid when you get payment. If you fail to do this, it may look like you have an outstanding balance, when you really do not.

When you know there are outstanding balances, it is important for you to create terms a client will want to stick to for making payments on time. You might implement such things as finance charges, which shows the client you are going to start charging interest if the money is not paid quickly. You can also set up "fees" that are not interest charges, but overdue payment fees that will make the client want to pay quicker. It is best that you develop a strict collection procedure with your clients.

The above is information for basic steps in recording revenues and assigning payments made to your company. You also have information with regards to keeping the money flowing in from customers. Part of basic operations in QuickBooks also includes recording expenses and paying the bills. We will assess those steps in part 2.

CHAPTER 7

BASIC STEPS TO OPERATING QUICKBOOKS – PART 2

Accounts Receivable is just a portion of the bookkeeping and accounting procedures you do daily. You also perform accounts payable functions, which can be split into two categories: recording expenses and bill paying.

Recording Expenses

Expenses for many companies are considered a different type of expenditure than accounts payable. Accounts payable is the term applied to short-term debt or money owed to your suppliers and creditors. For example, the liabilities you have such as vehicle loans, commercial loans, vendor and distributor payments to your suppliers and other revolving liabilities are under accounts payable.

Expenses are office supplies, energy bills, water bills and other utilities. Expenses can be things you pay for out of your personal pocket and reimburse yourself with, such as using paid outs or bill pay to write you a check for the amount spent.

Both types of business expenditures need to be recorded and allocated to an appropriate class or category. For example, you would label office supplies under the category office supplies, but include only things like paper, ink, pens, staples, and other simple items. Equipment such as new computers would be considered assets and not "supplies."

For typical operating expenses, you will usually pay those bills right away, but you still need to record the payments. With supplier and other creditor expenses, you may record the bills, but wait until you perform weekly tasks to pay the actual bill.

You want to keep track of what you need to pay and the terms behind those payments. Let's use an example. You are a distributor of a product. You import products from several manufacturers and then distribute them to your customers, who are vendors selling to multiple retail stores.

You pay for the products you import and bill customers for the products you distribute. In this scenario, you need to record each time you receive products by tracking the invoice number, payment terms, and whether you have paid the current invoice.

There are two choices you will make when it comes to bill paying. Are you going to pay now or later? You can always pay the invoice the minute you receive it, so you would record it and then set up to print the check for the invoice. You can also record the invoice, without paying it.

Paying a bill when it comes in is an excellent choice. You do everything at once and ensure nothing falls through the cracks. However, sometimes you need accounts receivable to be up-to-date to afford the large payments, which means you may need to wait to pay the bill, but you want to make sure you don't forget what you have to pay when.

Accounts payable method where you record the invoices and keep track of outstanding bills is often the most used method for businesses due to cash flow requirements.

Each step you want to perform is outlined below to help you record expenses and pay the bills.

Recording Bills

When you receive a bill, but are not ready to write the check, you want to record it.

1. Go to "Vendors."

2. Select "Enter Bills."

3. Choose the "vendor" the bill came from.

4. Enter the payment terms.

5. If you have a vendor reference number, you can enter it.

6. You can also record any memo for the bill, if necessary.

7. Go to the account column in the expenses tab and enter the expense account name.

8. Tab over to the amount column to enter the amount.

9. The items tab allows you to enter information about the bill, such as what you are paying for and how many you received.

10. Save the bill. You can "save and new" or if done "save and close."

Now that you have entered the bills, you have a record of what you are paying for or will pay for in the future. If you make a mistake, you can always delete the bill.

Go into the Accounts Payable register and select the bill you want to remove. Choose "edit" and then click "delete bill."

You also have the option of having QuickBooks remind you of the bills you need to pay. Go into Edit, Preferences, and click the "Reminders" icon which allows you to tell the program what you want reminders for, including paying bills.

The above information is about recording the bills as they come in, and not necessarily paying them. The next section will address further details about making payments.

Writing a Check

One method is paying bills by writing a check. Under this method, the invoice information ends up in the check register and happens simultaneously with creating checks. It is a slower method. Here are the steps:

1. Choose "Banking" from the menu.

2. Find "Write Checks" in the drop-down menu. (You can also click write checks in the banking section) A screen will open, where you have a check format on the top and the expenses and items tabs in the middle of the screen.

3. Choose the bank account you will use to make the payment.

4. Fill in the date.

5. Put a name in the Pay to the Order Of section.

6. Enter an amount for the payment.

7. You can add the address and a memo to the check if necessary.

8. In the Account column assign an expense to associate with the payment.

9. In the Item section you can list what you purchased with the payment being made.

10. When done entering all the pertinent details, click save, either "new" or "close."

Close the window and get out of check writing if you only need to do one check. If you have multiple payments to make, click "Save and New" to keep writing checks.

When you have completed your data entry and are ready to print the checks, you will need to select the option to print. More information will be provided for how to print the checks. It is not included here because you may perform the check printing option weekly instead of daily.

Quick Accounts Payable

1. Go to "Banking"

2. Select "Use Register"

3. Fill in the details for the check, including payee name, account, and the amount. You can also "split" the check to show it is for more than one expense.

4. When you are done entering the information click "record."

This method is mostly for expenses like the electricity bill. You can also use the slow method of writing a check for everyday business expenses. It is possible to write yourself a check as a way of reimbursing you for expenses you might have paid out of pocket or with your personal account. Under the quick accounts payable method, you have the option of transferring money from one business account to another should you need to reimburse an account for a payment made. As you can imagine there are plenty of things to learn about accounts payable methods.

Paying Bills Later

The reminder, you set up after you recorded the bills, tells you bills are in need of paying, so now you need to write the checks for the bills you entered.

1. From "Vendors" choose "Pay Bills."

2. Enter a Payment Date for the checks.

3. Set a date to show only the bills that need paying.

4. Use "sort" to help you sort the bills.

5. Identify which bills you intend on paying.

6. If necessary, such as to make a partial payment, change the amount.

7. Select the payment date, method, and bank account.

8. Select the "To be Printed" option to ensure you can print the checks.

9. Click "Pay Selected Bills."

Once you click pay selected bills they will be marked as paid and you can print the checks to mail. If something goes wrong with printing the checks, you can tell the system to print them again. It will give you easy to follow prompts to make sure everything worked out as it should with regards to printing checks and marking bills paid.

Printing Checks

1. Go to "File"

2. "Printer Setup"

3. Select "Check/Paycheck"

4. From the Printer Name list select the printer

5. Select the printer type if you need to.

6. Select the check style

7. Click printer setup if you need to change the font.

8. Click "OK" to finish.

You are now ready to start printing checks as you write them or later when you are paying bills.

If you are printing as you write the checks, you just need to click print in the "Write Checks" window.

If you are printing multiple checks, you will go to the register, mark the checks you want to print and then go to File, Print Forms, Checks, and print the checks you want.

The above information provides the basic details you need for recording your bills, paying the bills now or later, and how to print checks when you are ready to make the payments. You may perform the actual check printing once a week, but for those who want it as part of the daily tasks, you have the steps included with the daily tasks of entering bills and potentially making those payments.

Paying Electronically

Many companies, including energy companies, are making it possible to pay bills electronically instead of writing and printing checks. Whether you want to use a credit card to make the payments to reap the rewards of air miles or you want to use ACH payments, you can do so through QuickBooks.

Remember, when you set up the bank accounts? Well, you have imputed all the information you need to make a payment with your bank account. You just tie it with the company you are making the bill payment to and tell QuickBooks you made an electronic payment versus writing a check. As you create the bills to pay, you assign the payment type. It is as simple as following the prompts and associating the correct categories and payment type in the check register and accounts payable sections.

CHAPTER 8

BASIC STEPS TO OPERATING QUICKBOOKS – PART 3

Another part of operating your business is to ensure your bank accounts are reconciled. Balancing the checkbook requires you to perform functions like ensuring the checkbook details are up-to-date daily or weekly, and that you are recording the deposits, as much as you record the revenue and expenses. Deposits and QuickBooks are made when you actually take the money to the bank. You will also learn about using credit cards as part of your payment method of expenses you have in your company. The credit card information is separate from paying the bills because it is away for you to pay for goods or services on credit rather than a straight payment or supplier invoice.

Deposits in QuickBooks

The type of business you have will determine how much cash inflow you have and when you need to do deposits. The typical business has three deposits to record.

1. Cash sales

2. Credit Card sales

3. Invoice payments

Any retail company or hospitality industry will need to record their daily deposits. If the company also invoices their customers, such as invoicing a library for books bought from a bookstore, the money will be recorded as an invoice payment and needs to be deposited.

The bookkeeper has the responsibility daily, weekly, or monthly to record the incoming money and making sure the bank account tied to QuickBooks shows the deposits.

Making the deposits puts the money recorded from sales and customer payments as deposited instead of "un-deposited funds."

1. Go to "Banking."

2. Choose "Make Deposits."

3. Select the payments you are depositing.

4. Click "Ok."

5. Choose the Bank Account the deposits are going into.

6. Choose the correct deposit date.

Click on "Save and Close" or make a new deposit.

Your checkbook details are now accurately showing the cash, checks, and credit card income you received.

Note that when you pay a bill and write the check, you update the checkbook details to reflect the outflow of money.

Business Credit Cards

Another area that you need to focus on is if you pay with credit cards for business expenses. The arrangement of credit card expenses as part of the checkbook details is due to tracking things like the funds that are going out as part of a "petty cash" option. Some companies keep petty cash on hand, while others simply use paid outs to take the money from the daily sales cash, and others track everything on credit cards. You know how to show an individual expense by paying a bill. You may still want to keep the expenses on a credit card as individual transactions. For example, if the card is used for fuel and meals, you may want to record the fuel as a separate expense for the month from the meals.

You can also decide that the "credit card" bill you pay is enough to show that there are expenses to record for the outflow of money. If you wish to tie a credit card to QuickBooks as a means of using the credit card to pay for expenses and recording the information in QuickBooks, then you will want to set up a credit card account.

1. Go to "Chart of Accounts"
2. Click the Account Button on the screen and choose "New."
3. Select "Credit Card"

4. Put a name in for the account, such as who uses the card or the credit card company.

5. Type the card number into the Credit Card Account Number box.

6. Save and close.

The reason you may wish to do this as a way to keep your "checkbook" details is because you are actually able to enter each transaction you have made using the credit card. In fact, like the Check Register, you now have a Credit Card Register.

In Banking:

1. Select "Enter Credit Card Charges"

2. From the drop-down menu choose the credit card account

3. In the purchased from field enter the place you used the credit card.

4. Indicate if it was a purchase or credit.

5. Enter the date.

6. Type the amount.

7. If necessary, use a memo to add more information.

8. Fill in the expense's category.

9. Put the itemized breakdown of the information.

10. Record by hitting save and new or save and close.

If you need to, you can edit or void a credit card transaction you put in the register.

- Go to Chart of Accounts
- Find the credit card account
- Choose the transaction to delete, edit, or void.
- Save your changes.

Like the check register, you will eventually learn how to reconcile the accounts to ensure you and the company are matching for payments made on the account and charges made. As you saw in the instructions, you can record a payment you make to the credit card account instead of making it a purchase. The credit function lets you record the payments you made to the account; thus, you will balance with the statement when it comes in. Also, by recording the transaction in the check register and as a credit for payment made to the credit card, you will balance in both registers.

Other daily tasks include updating your inventory information, ordering more, and reconciling what you sold. However, before talking about inventory, you should understand the basic steps to payroll. While it is often a weekly, bi-weekly, or semi-monthly task, it is something you do frequently and is of highest importance to your employees. You need to know how to do this function immediately to keep your employees paid on time.

CHAPTER 9

PAYROLL EXPLAINED

Employees want their checks on the date promised. If you have hand-written checks or outsourced this procedure, you no longer need to do so because QuickBooks will do everything for you.

During the set-up phase, you learned how to enter employees into QuickBooks, assign their withholding details, and set up payroll taxes. Now, you are going to use the features by creating paychecks.

There are two ways to create paychecks. You can pay for the payroll service QuickBooks offers. It helps you automatically assign the tax information. It will also calculate each employee tax details to create the paycheck accordingly. QuickBooks has a manual payroll function, if you do not want to pay for the added service.

The one thing QuickBooks is not going to do is direct deposit. For direct deposit options, you need an accountant that has ADP or Paychex for their clients or sign up for those services.

If you want to use the online resource from QuickBooks be prepared to pay $200 or $500 per year. The basic service will help with the checks, but you still do the work of filing the payroll taxes. The more advanced version will help with payroll forms and checks.

For companies that have fewer than 15 employees, there is no reason to pay out the $200 per year or even more. Doing the payroll manually takes less than 30 minutes, even if you are imputing all the tax deductions for each check.

There are some steps that will help you ensure the right information is provided, such as entering all the withholding information and setting up the payroll schedule. If necessary, go back into each employee and make certain you have it set up for regular hours, and the payment periods you prefer, such as weekly, semi-monthly, or bi-weekly. You can also choose monthly.

1. On the screen, find the employees section or use the menus to open Employees and then "Pay Employees."

2. Check the pay period end date is correct.

3. Check the date that will be on the check is right.

4. Click on the employees who you are creating paychecks for, you might have some part-time employees who are not being paid each time but are active.

5. Once all employees are check-marked, click "open paycheck details."

6. In this section, you can add hours, check the date range, and manually enter the tax information for this pay period. (You may need to do this if you have not paid for the QuickBooks service or set up the tax details for each employee).

7. After all paychecks are accurate with date, hours, and taxes, save and close.

8. Click "create paychecks."

9. Review the information.

10. Print the checks, there are a couple of steps to printing, so follow the prompts, and if something does not print correctly, you can tell it to reprint certain checks or all checks.

It is easier if you have the tax information set up in QuickBooks even if you are manually entering the employee hours or not using the online service. However, it is not the end of the world if you want to take more time to create paychecks, it does mean you will need to have an accountant help you with your tax liabilities regarding payroll.

Pay Tax Liabilities

If you have payroll set up with tax information, you can manually go into Employees, and Payroll Taxes and Liabilities.

From this section you will click the payroll liability you are paying and click "view/pay." It will create a check and put it in the register, you can also print the check.

Unless you pay for the payroll service, you are not going to find the quarterly and annual returns and wage statements are available to you. You may also have to calculate your tax liabilities outside the program.

These features are something you want to consider, weigh the costs of from an accountant standpoint, and determine if paying for QuickBooks basic or full service is worth the help provided.

The one thing you do not want to do is forget to make the Federal and State payments required for the payroll. Small companies often benefit from manually creating the checks in house but letting an accountant deal with the tax side of things.

QuickBooks and Employee Hours

The above discussion and how-to manually create paychecks, assumes your employees do not use the employee hour function in QuickBooks. Make sure you have the QuickBooks plan that includes time tracking.

Freelance or self-employed versions do not, but the Pro, and above software programs do

1. Go to the Gear Icon on the Toolbar (in the online version)

2. Under Company, go to Account and Settings

3. Select "Advanced"

4. Go to "Time Tracking"

5. Set your preferences, such as timesheets or billable to a certain customer.

6. Select Save and close out.

You also need to add users for time tracking, so your employees can "punch in."

1. Since you are still in the Company area after you close the "advanced settings, go to Manage Users.

2. Select Add User

3. Select Time Tracking Only

4. Next

5. Select the employees to add

6. Save

You can decide to make the time billable, which would ensure you allocate the time spent on projects and jobs to a specific customer. This is helpful if you have a service business like a construction company and need to show the customer the hours worked.

You can also have the option of creating a report for time tracking, which would show the activities based on the employees so you can pay them for the time they worked. This function is under the "reports" menu in your QuickBooks program.

Your employees will need to go into the time tracker to sign on and off for work. Employees should login and access their weekly or bi-weekly timesheet.

1. Under Employees, you will go to Enter Time and create the timesheet based on your pay period.

2. Create one for each employee by going to their name in the drop-down menu.

3. Have the employee enter their hours each day.

4. Save and close.

When you are ready to do the payroll, you can then access the timesheets and have the hours appear in the create paycheck area. This helps you electronically record the hours worked, calculate the taxes to deduct, and then write the checks using QuickBooks. You will want to review the weekly timesheets, either by accessing the report or by looking at every person individually. As the person making the paychecks, you want to ensure your employees have entered the correct data before you make the paychecks. It becomes more complicated if someone forgets to add their hours appropriately.

You would have to enter the data for the next pay period but assign it correctly as regular income. You do have the function to add in overtime, vacation, and sick pay. These options, if you supply them to your employees, would need to be noted under their employee profile and then as you enter their hours you would allocate everything appropriately.

Remember you have tutorials you can view online, if you need to discover more about payroll entering, including how to update employee information such as changes to vacation time, personal days, and overtime.

In the employee section, when you edit your employee information you can change their wages as you provide raises. You need to update any changes to their hours or wages, prior to creating the checks. If you do not remember to adjust the wagers or hours, you can do so manually, but you should remember to go in and make those adjustments before you create checks the next time.

CHAPTER 10

INVENTORY TASKS

For some companies, inventory is a part of the business. Even for companies that offer services, keeping track of inventory can be helpful. As an example, we will discuss an internet service provider. The ISP has routers, modems, connection wires, and may have wireless equipment for "access points" that project the Internet signal to multiple customers rather than operating on fiber optic wire. Such a company would need to keep track of the access point equipment and the internet equipment they rent or sell to the customer. While, the inventory might be small, compared to a bookstore that could have thousands of books, the business still needs to keep up with inventory.

You will need to track inventory, keep up with inventory as you purchase and sell items, use purchase orders to help track it, and adjust what you have in stock versus what it shows is in stock. If you have more than one business location, you may need to keep track of inventory for multiple locations.

Setting up Inventory

You need to tell QuickBooks you want to track inventory.

- Go to Edit
- Preferences
- Select "Items and Inventory"
- Check "Inventory and Purchase Orders" is active.
- You can also tell QuickBooks to warn you if you do not have enough inventory.

Next, you will need to create an item list. Any items you intend to have in your inventory need to be on this list. You should set up the initial list and as you buy new inventory, you can add new items as you create purchase orders. You will keep updating your item list to help you track the inventory. You have the option of deleting things you cannot get again or do not want, as well as adding new products that you wish to bring in to your store.

Buying Stuff and Inventory

Creating a PO when you make an order is the best way to update your inventory. However, there are times when you may buy things in person and pay for them at the time or receive a bill in the mail. It would mean there is no purchase order in the system.

Let's say you bought a few items at a show and you are being billed later.

1. Go to Vendors

2. Receive Items

3. Receive Inventory

4. Select Receive Inventory without a Bill

5. Fill in the information for the vendor, if it is a new vendor make sure you add them.

6. Click the "items" tab

7. In the columns begin adding information about the product

8. Add in the quantity and your costs

9. Click "save and new" or close if there is nothing else to add.

Since you received the items and created a PO, you can go into the vendors area, click on enter bills for received items, and ensure you make the payment to the company.

If you have the item and the bill, you can enter everything all at once.

You still go to vendors:

1. Click Receive Items and Enter Bill.

2. Fill out the information for the vendor.

3. Go to the Items tab and start adding the details.

4. Save the information and either create a new one or close out of the area.

There are also times when you need to record the stuff you sell. Your inventory is in a constant flux of adding new items and selling what you have. Anytime you make a sale and it is recorded in QuickBooks through the Point-of-Sale system or with a sales receipt, your inventory will adjust. You don't have to update your inventory record because you record the sale in some way to indicate the sale has occurred, and what type of tender was given for the sale.

Creating Purchase Orders

While on the discussion of inventory and receiving new items, it is a clever idea to consider how to create the purchase orders for those orders you make. The advantage of QuickBooks is you don't need to use Excel or Word to create a document to fax or email to the companies you order from—you can use QuickBooks purchase orders, and let the software do the work for you.

It is important to add any new vendor you may order from prior to creating a purchase order.

1. Go to Vendor

2. Click "Create Purchase Orders"

3. Choose the correct vendor from the list.

4. Choose the inventory items you want to order; you can do this through the "class" list.

5. You can also start typing the item name in the item column and things will appear for you to choose.

6. Enter the item and the quantity.

7. If you need to add a memo in the memo field.

8. Click print to get a copy

9. Click save and new or close out of the PO area when you are done.

You will have the option of choosing how you want to submit the order, whether you do so electronically or call it in.

As with any other task in QuickBooks there are ways to ensure you get reminders when you need them. You may forget about an order because it is a busy time of year and you can go back in to see if you have received against all PO's created and if not, you can start looking into what happened. The fact that you have reports and reminders that help you check on things, as well as the option of going into the PO and adding things a day or so later, ensures you keep on top of your company business.

For companies that have multiple locations, you are better off with setting up multiple companies with QuickBooks and telling the program which location you want to work with for orders and other data sets. It is not easy to have more than one location's inventory tracked, unless you set up item numbers based on locations or you have multiple company details set up for your business.

Remember, QuickBooks is not set up for large businesses with more than 50 employees or multiple locations selling inventory. It works for service-oriented companies because you pay employees, bring in revenue, but don't have to track inventory.

CHAPTER 11

BUDGETING

The three financial reports, income statement, statement of cash flows, and balance sheet are designed to help you correct issues with your company's operations and to help you budget for the next quarter or year. The financial reports offer insight into trends, which help you determine if you need to order supplies. Creating the budget is considered an occasional task because you may make changes as things happen throughout the year to reallocate funds from one area to cover another expense. It falls under the occasional tasks along with the discussion on printing checks and payroll. It is a task that will require housekeeping tasks before it can be performed.

Going back to our bookstore example for a moment, consider if it is the only store in town and in a tourist community. The main period of sales would be during the height of the tourist season. It would be correct to assume the shop orders more books for the increase in customers and fewer during the off season. But one also has to account for whether each year will see the same influx of tourists. If information shows a year on year increase for the last two years, the trend will likely continue, unless economic strains occur throughout the country or world. The black and white financial reports help someone assess past and current trends, while also helping in the decision-making process for whether to allocate funds to different departments.

The budget comes in when you decide if your company has areas of struggle or is in a good situation, and whether you want to improve business with more or less advertising, carrying fewer or more items, and ensuring you maintain your budget.

We will discuss another example. We will say a piece of equipment breaks down in the first quarter. The budget for that department has to use two quarters worth of their budget, which puts a strain on the next quarter. Using the budget and financial reports, a company can decide if changes should be made to other departments to cover the large and unforeseen expense.

Creating the budget is something you do each year at the beginning of the year. You also have the option of amending it each quarter. To set up a budget go to planning and budgeting in the company section.

Budget Steps

1. Click set up budget

2. Select the year you are budgeting.

3. Select the type of budget you want to establish. You have an option of creating an income and expense budget or a budget of year-end asset, liability, and equity balances. Once you input for a budget income statement amounts or balance sheet amounts, click next.

4. Provide the information requested by the software.

5. If you want to start a new budget or start with last year's numbers, you can. Make your choice and choose finish.

6. Start entering budget information for the departments you plan to allocate funds to and once you are done save the work.

You can go into the budget and adjust it as needed. QuickBooks allows you to forecast profits and losses, project cash flows, and plan for things that may come up for income or expenses.

It is up to you to decide what types of items will go into the budget. You may have advertising, office supplies, inventory, wages, taxes, and related categories listed on your budget.

Tips for Budgeting

- Assign each expense and income a class in QuickBooks. You want to make sure everything has a category for the type of expense it is.

- Each month you will have different expenses; however, the categories these expenses fall into need to fit the quarterly budget. For example, you may not have office supplies each month because you buy in bulk. Yet, you want to make certain you have a budget category set up and assigned an amount.

- List all debts the company has, including any loans that are currently in repayment. Certain debts may be paid each month, like the employee credit card.

- It is best to assess the budget on a quarterly basis to see where you may need to reassign funds or cut expenses. Do not be afraid to find deals on office supplies, cut back your employee's meals, and other areas when you have more important expenses to worry about.

- Your budget is meant to be a schedule of payments, which includes the invoice terms you are responsible for throughout the year.

- The previous years' need to help you create a buffer for a change in sales or services. In a business, you never know what may occur in terms of economic downturns or upturns. Your budget is meant to keep you on track to cover your costs and employee payments. You also have to project expenses like replacement vehicles, computers, and other equipment. It is possible to run on a deficit in one quarter and positive in another.

- The key is to ensure you are running in the black for the year, whether you have some months at a deficit.

If you are a freelancer or work on commissions, things will differ slightly. Freelancers may pay commissions to get outside work accomplished, but they rarely have employees. Your budget is usually dependent on the amount of work you do, with few assets.

Freelancers like writers, artists, and other services usually work from home. You can have a home-based service business, such as commercial kitchen equipment repair. You have few inventory items you use to replace parts, typically, you order the parts needed when you need them. Your job is contingent on something breaking down or needing its maintenance, as per the manufacturer's maintenance schedule. In situations like these, it is harder to budget on a quarterly basis. However, you should still have a plan for your company.

- Marketing and advertising expenses should increase when work is slow.

- Even if you are not being paid, you need to find ways to ensure you get more work coming your way.

- You have to sell yourself more.

A function of QuickBooks is to tie in with hosting a website. If you decide you want to add a package with hosting services, you can create an ecommerce or services website, and use social media tie-ins to prompt your company.

When work is slow, you need to work harder to market your skills, not only locally, but globally depending on what your skills are.

It becomes a budget more about time than incoming funds. However, you also need to realize what you make one month may need to carry you through a lean month or five. For this reason, keeping on top of the budget, correcting the forecasting for a better projection of income, and saving money when it matters is necessary.

Freelances may work their budget each month, which is fine and possible with QuickBooks. The added benefit of the online freelancer program is to have a software program geared more towards your potential income and help you budget more appropriately based on those monthly expenses you must pay.

If you are unsure what budget categories to use, consult an accountant. Your accountant will have what they call a "Chart of Accounts" which is how you allocate your income and expenses. The categories your accountant uses are based on the deductions your business can take. Meals and entertainment are consolidated into one category. Vehicle mileage is another category.

From the above tips and discussion, you should have a good understanding of budget topics, why budgeting is important, and how it differs for the freelance or commission style work.

CHAPTER 12

FINANCIAL REPORTING WITH QUICKBOOKS

Reports are usually part of the housekeeping tasks you are going to perform. The financial reports listed here are something you print for the budget, taxes, and to keep around for the government audits. There are more housekeeping tasks to discuss after you learn how to print the main three financial reports.

QuickBooks provides reports to help companies check on the business' health. Balance sheets, statement of cash flow, income statements, and other reports are available for you to print and check. How often you look at these reports is up to you. You should make them part of the occasional business you take care of as the bookkeeper/owner. The type of reports you want to print will also depend on the business you run. The steps to create these individual reports and others you might find useful are examined in this chapter. Remember, you have training and QuickBooks help to use should you find there are reports you need that are not listed in this section.

Before you print reports or decide they are imperative to your company's operations, you need to know what they are, why you need them, and then you can learn how to create them.

Balance Sheet

The balance sheet is a statement showing assets, capital, and liabilities. It is helpful to balance your income and expenditures for specific periods, such as quarterly health checks. If you want to know how the business is doing, what it made for the quarter, and how high your expenditures are to improve your company's health, a balance sheet is a place to start. You will gain information about your assets, what the company owes, and its overall net worth. The QuickBooks balance sheet is organized into two sections, so you can see what you have with what you owe subtracted. Together with the income statement and statement of cash flow, you can spot trends in your company, particularly, with customers paying you and whether you can pay your bills.

How to Create the Balance Sheet

First, you need to make a choice regarding the type of report you want for the Balance Sheet. The standard report will show the information we have discussed for a specific date. Detailed sheets add to the information for a month period with a beginning and ending balance for the specified month. A summary Balance Sheet has only the ending balances for all the accounts instead of each individual account. You can also create a year on year comparison or set a specific class for the report, such as assigning all the income and expenses to specific expense categories.

1. In the File menu, choose Reports.

2. Chose Company and Financial in the reports drop-down menu.

3. Chose the type of Balance Sheet.

4. Print it if you want or save it to your computer.

Statement of Cash Flow

The statement of cash flow will summarize the cash and assets that enter and leave the business. Combined with the balance sheet and income statement, businesses need to print these reports for the year. It was made a mandatory part of financial records in 1987. The cash flow statement helps a company see how it is running, where the money is coming from, and how much is spent. It is also a way to see how much cash is available for operating expenses and whether a company can pay its debts. The idea behind the cash flow statement is to help with investors or help creditors see the health of a company. The cash flow statement will typically show cash, accounts receivable, accounts payable, depreciation of equipment, and inventory. The cash flow statement uses information from the balance sheet and income statement to populate.

The statement made through QuickBooks will have six pieces of information:

- Operations
- Cash balance
- Finance
- Investing
- New cash balance
- Forecasting

You can create the statement with the direct or indirect method. The direct method will show in and out flows of money by subtracting the money spent from what was received. The indirect method begins with the net income and factors in things like depreciation.

1. From file or the left-side menu, select reports.

2. Find the statement of cash flows.

3. Select it to open it.

4. Customize the report for what you may need, such as putting in a date range for the report period.

5. Run report

6. Print the report, if necessary.

Income Statement

You can create different reports for income statements, like the profit and loss statement. If you want the full version of the income statement, go to the reports area in your version of the program and search for the statement you want. Some consider the profit and loss statement to be the income statement. Both are going to show the revenue and expenses for the period you choose to help you focus on your company's performance. There will usually be four items of information on the full report: expenses, revenue, gains, and losses. If you want to, you can just show the profit and loss, without the revenue and expenses, but with a net revenue provided.

The reason you want this statement is to show the net income, total revenue, and see if your company is performing correctly, managed right, or if there are areas that are underperforming.

1. Choose income statement from the search results.

2. Customize the statement for the dates, columns, notes, reason, and other items.

3. Run the report.

4. Save it to your computer and print it.

A Profit and Loss Statement

1. From reports, choose company and financial.

2. Choose profit and loss standard.

3. You can modify the report to show up to 12 months of data.

4. You can also select total only or month.

5. Ok

6. Print, if you need to.

CHAPTER 13

BALANCING THE CHECK REGISTER

Daily tasks are about recording information. Occasional tasks keep you on point for ensuring payments are made, reminders are sent, and you are on budget. Housekeeping tasks are often drudgery. You don't want to do them, but you need to, and they are where it matters if you are a good bookkeeper. If you are sloppy in your work, leaving bills to be entered, invoices have paid, and lack the task management to enter all data as it comes in, then balancing your check register is difficult.

It should be easy. Balancing the check register is actually so simple compared to the old method of manually checking your written register against the bank statement, you shouldn't fear it. If you maintain your records correctly, you will not have to explain the differences between the two accounts, unless it has to do with checks you wrote, but they did not clear before the bank statement.

The Steps for Balancing

1. Under Banking, select reconcile

2. Choose the bank account.

3. Put in the statement date

4. Verify the opening balance

5. Enter the ending balance from your bank statement

6. Enter any bank fees, plus the date

7. Enter any interest income, if any and the date it occurred

8. Continue

The first thing you want to do is mark any deposits that cleared. If you see a deposit on the statement that is not in QuickBooks, it means you did not enter the record of the deposit. You should record it now.

Make sure you mark each deposit that has cleared and entered any that you did not do prior to balancing the check register. Once you have marked all deposits, it is time to find all the checks that cleared.

9. Find the first check that has cleared and mark it as such.

10. Record any check you see on your bank statement, but that did not show up in the check register for QuickBooks.

11. Continue with these steps until you have all the checks from your bank statement marked as cleared and entered in QuickBooks.

At this point, you should see a difference between the cleared balance and ending balance as zero. However, if there are things you missed or accidentally selected, you may see a balance that is different than zero. You would need to go back through to find the error. You can also click reconcile now and it will show you a box opening the adjustment window.

In that window you can attempt to find the error or enter an adjustment to reconcile. Once you are done, return to reconcile. For those who show zero, just reconcile the account and you are done.

There are some typical reasons you might not reconcile between your bank statement and QuickBooks.

- You have a transaction the bank has not processed yet, but you select it as cleared.

- You did not enter something the bank statement has or forgot to select clear.

- A reversed transaction occurred, whether by design or accident, and now you need to correct the issue or wait for the bank to show the correction.

- You have a transaction that was partially made, and you forgot to go in and reflect the partial payment or the full payment when it happened.

- You might have transposed numbers.

- You definitely want to look for anything that matches the exact amount you are off, but do not forget it could be more than one transaction error.

- You can click "locate discrepancies" to help you.

- Have a second person checking your work.

- Leave it for this month and try to reconcile correctly next month. You might find a transaction you thought cleared and did not.

The beauty of being linked with your bank accounts are that you can reconcile with online statements. You can import your statement from your bank during the reconciliation of the check register, which allows it to automatically find the transactions by amount, check number, and other information.

It works by automatically assigning bank statement information to what is shown in your check register. At the end of the process, it will tell you if there are items not in the check register, but on the bank statement. At this point, you get a chance to add them to your QuickBooks program, so that you reconcile perfectly.

The process described in the chapter is primarily for those who do not import their bank statements but do things in a non-online capacity.

For those who keep up with entering payments, deposits, and other revenue daily or weekly, it should take a couple minutes to reconcile the check register and move on.

CHAPTER 14

REPORTS

As part of the occasional tasks, you may want to run a variety of reports to check on your business' performance. There are numerous reports QuickBooks provides. All it takes is knowing what each report is, how it can help you, and how to print it. We have already talked about the three main financial reports, but there are more options like sales tax and other tax reports. The following is a list of the reports you can access in QuickBooks.

- Customers and Receivables – reports designed to help you track customer invoices. The report can list unpaid invoices, organize them by customer, job, or length of time it is outstanding.

- Sales – reports that show you who your customers are and what you have sold. The sales reports can be broken down by item, sales rep, and customer.

- Time and Mileage – for each job you have, you can run a report for the time spent on the job and any vehicle mileage required to complete the job. Under these reports you get to see the profitability, estimate comparison to actual costs, time and functions completed, and vehicle mileage.

- Purchases – designed to show who, what, and how regarding items you purchased for the store. You are able to customize the reports by vendor or item. You also have purchase order reports that show any outstanding orders to help you track what has arrived and what is still incoming.

- Inventory – as with purchase orders, you can use this report to track what you have on hand, what you sell the most of, and then design a new purchase order based on what your business needs to order.

- Vendors and Payables – the account payable reports are designed to help you pay your bills. The report can list everything by vendor or oldest unpaid first. There is also a report for sales tax liability generated once you know what is paid or unpaid.

- Employees and Payroll – tracking what your employees are doing, what you have paid for, and therefore your tax liability is imperative, so the three reports for employees and payroll are essential to your company's operations.

- Accountant and Taxes – like other tax liabilities, you need to track tax reports, general ledger reports, journal reports, and trial balance information, which the accountant and taxes reports help you do.

- Banking – if you ever need a bank statement based on QuickBooks, it can be found in the banking reports.

- Budget and Forecasts – how do you know your quarter or year was on target or where the breakdown occurred? The reports that print the budget, your forecasts, and assess whether you are on target.

- List – report lists will show contacts, customer, vendor, and other name-oriented lists, which can help with inventory particulars.

- Industry Specific – depending on your version of QuickBooks you may have reports that are helpful to your business type. Some QuickBooks versions have reports for accountants, manufacturers, contractors, wholesalers, retailers, nonprofits, and professional service firms.

- Contributed Reports – provides access to custom report templates from Intuit and other companies that may help you generate reports you require for your business.

- Custom – Like contributed reports, custom options help you customize summary and transaction reports.

Knowing the reports are available in QuickBooks is just the beginning. Creating the report and printing it is essential.

Creating Reports

All the reports will be housed in the "reports" menu. In the drop-down menu, you will need to select the report you want. When it opens to the report options screen, there are ways to customize the report to fit the dates and information you want from it.

Click the "ok" option to get the report to generate. It will appear on screen. If you do not want to print, you can use your arrow keys to move up and down. It allows you to view the various parts of the report on screen.

For those who want to print the report, click on the print icon at the top of the report. The print dialogue box will appear and from there you can choose the correct printer, and then print the report.

There are other benefits to creating the reports, such as exporting the report into an Excel or .CSV file. Sometimes, reports are set up to best-fit all QuickBooks users, which might include information you do not want. By exporting to a file, you are able to edit and rearrange the report.

QuickBooks does provide options in the program to edit and rearrange some of the information. For example, you can click on customize report, share template, comment, memorize, email, Excel, and more. If you have more than one person in the company who will use the report, then sharing it is a helpful option. Memorize is also a way to share a report to a group.

Sometimes you need to turn on functions in QuickBooks to make use of a report. Job information is one of those functions.

Job Estimating, Billing, and Tracking

Before you can generate reports and monitor how jobs are going, you must turn on those functions in the program.

1. In Edit, select Preferences

2. Click Jobs and Estimates

3. Go to Company Preferences Tab

4. Select Yes to tell it you want to create estimates and progress invoices

Progress invoices are those you provide to the customer to gain money during an ongoing job. For example, you may receive an amount of money upfront for materials to build a house. A month later, you might bill another chunk of money for the progress you made, and at the end you settle up what is left.

Once you have the functions in place, you need to understand how you set up the job, create the estimates, and track the billing information.

Job: The Set Up

To track the invoices and costs, you need to set the job up in QuickBooks. In fact, before you can create an estimate, you need to tell the system you have a new potential job.

- Under Customers, go to Customer Center
- Enter a new customer or choose one from the list
- Add job
- Enter the details of the new job

With the set up complete, you are ready to create the job estimate.

- In Customers, select Create Estimates
- Fill in the blanks for the job form, which is in the drop-down list.
- Add as many details as required
- Save and close it.

You can come back to the estimate when you learn more information about the job. For example, you might not have the cost of an item needed for the work. If you have a construction company and are estimating the cost to build a house, you might need to research a couple of windows, flooring, cabinet, and other companies. You may also be waiting for estimates from sub-contractors on things like concrete, foundation work, plumbing, and electric. You are always able to go into the customer job file and revise the estimate.

Once you have submitted the estimate to your customer and it has been approved, you can go into QuickBooks and turn the estimate into the invoice. If there are any changes you and the customer agreed to make now is the time to edit the estimate one final time before you complete the steps to turn it into an invoice.

1. In the Customer Center, find the customer and open the screen.

2. A list of estimates appears, click on the one you want to work with.

3. Click the "Create Invoice" option.

4. You still have a last chance to make modifications.

5. Save and close or go to a new estimate.

As with any job where you are estimating the cost of the time, work, and products, there are times when the estimate and the actual cost may differ. QuickBooks allows you to compare the estimated and actual costs to show your customer why you might need to charge a little more or where you were able to help save them money. This ties back to the reports we discussed above about jobs.

When the amounts differ from the estimate and actual, you want to charge everything appropriately and in a way that looks professional. Open customers and create invoices. Find the correct customer.

When the screen opens, you are able to click on add time and costs. You will be able to enter the billable time and costs the job has and if necessary, you can add a markup. As you complete the changes, click okay and then save and close.

Under jobs in the time and mileage reports, you track the costs and are also able to print the reports, as mentioned earlier, to help you show the customer what is happening with their job.

Reports are your friend. When you walk into a bank for a construction loan to build spec houses, remodel homes for resale, or any number of reasons your specific business may have, reports will show how healthy your company is.

You benefit from the information because you can also see where you may need to make changes in employees, costs, and other business-related expenses. Some reports may be helpful for your accountant, but many of them are for you to interpret.

CHAPTER 15

HOW TO USE QUICKBOOKS EFFICIENTLY

Adding QuickBooks to your business can save you a lot of time. It can help you determine the health of your company, but you do want to use it in the most effective way. Whatever is going to save you time and allow your focus to be on bringing in more revenue is worth it. But how worth it is up to you. As you learned in payroll, you can do everything manually and take thirty minutes to an hour creating paychecks. You can also pay $200 per month to make it easier. It is possible to have an accountant come, set it up for the tax information, and ensure creating paychecks is simpler. The decisions are up to you; however, this guide can give you the "why" for whether you want to change current procedures or keep some of the old concepts.

In a discussion of efficiency, it should be noted that technology can fail us. If a storm knocks out the power, you are now back in the pre-tech days where everything was done by hand. A bit ago someone told a co-worker about a shop that got rid of its old knuckle cruncher—a credit card machine—using carbon paper to record numbers. The old-fashioned device was called "obsolete" and not worth keeping. For those who think about technology failing, it seems silly to call it obsolete. But, consider the majority of credit cards today—many are no longer embossed—meaning the numbers are not raised, so the machine cannot record the numbers on the carbon paper. For those cards, such a machine is obsolete, but for the embossed cards—it still works.

You want to think about efficiency in your company, but don't go too far in the other direction. If someone has a gift certificate for your store and the computer POS system is not working due to a power outage—it is great if you can go to a hard copy of those gift certificates to record the information until you can enter it in the POS system.

Hire an Accountant

Hiring an accountant is worthwhile depending on how many employees you have, the job duties required, and your knowledge. Not everyone is an accountant. Some of the simple things are easy to understand, but you are not going to research the tax law changes that happen each year. You are not going to have time, as a business owner, to keep up with certain accounting procedures.

There are several reasons to have an accountant. The best part is you can pay your accountant for the work they do, without hiring a full-time person, in your small business.

Larger small businesses may have the budget for an accountant/bookkeeper and that is worthwhile, if you can afford the person.

Hire a Bookkeeper

Some businesses have an accountant they use for the important projects, such as payroll taxes, Federal and State taxes in April. You can also hire a bookkeeper to come in to conduct occasional and housekeeping tasks. The person would enter information, print reports, and file for you. They could also create paychecks.

If you have a person on staff that is a manager or who has worked with QuickBooks in a management capacity, you could assign bookkeeper duties to that person.

By hiring an accountant or bookkeeper, or one person to fill both shoes, you are freed up to do more important business concepts. It ensures you are using QuickBooks efficiently because you are using your people effectively.

Shortcuts for QuickBooks

There are plenty of things you can do in two or more ways with QuickBooks, such as using the upper toolbar to find the drop-down menus, using the side menu display, or the main panel that says, company, reports, and employees. The cheats in this section are ways to use the keyboard to access or perform certain QuickBooks functions. If you are a mouse lover, then these may convert you to using the keyboard, since it can be a time-saving factor.

- To save a transaction: ALT S
- Save and move to new: ALT N
- Open the chart of accounts: CTRL A
- Copying items: CTRL C
- Deleting items like a check: CTRL D
- Editing register info: CTRL E
- Display search window: CTRL F
- Opening Create Invoice: CTRL I
- Create New: CTRL N
- To print: CTRL P
- To create and display a quick report: CTRL Q
- TO open the register window: CTRL R
- Pasting copied items: CTRL V
- To write checks: CTRL W
- Undo: CTRL Z
- Save Changes: CTRL Enter
- Inserting a new line: CTRL Insert
- To close a window or QuickBooks: ESC

These are just a few of the quicker ways you can perform actions in QuickBooks using your keyboard, rather than the mouse.

CHAPTER 16

HELPFUL SELF-EMPLOYED TAX DEDUCTIONS FOR SMALL BUSINESSES

Owning a small business makes you want to save as much money on expenses as possible. It can be hard because many of the deductions for taxes are disappearing. Thankfully, things change, so what you may not like in the coming years regarding tax deductions could change after another few years. As you struggle with finding deductions or realizing some things are not worth tracking anymore due to tax law changes, keep in mind the following information. Mileage, meals, and home-based deductions are still worthwhile for now. Your accountant can help you or your use of TurboTax through Intuit. QuickBooks can pair with TurboTax to help you maintain the proper tax filings, even without an accountant, at least if you are a self-employed person with few employees or working out of your home.

You do not want to miss the benefits provided, given how small they are.

Mileage Tax Deduction

Mileage is still one of the biggest deductions you can take on your IRS filings. In 2018, it was announced there would be a "standard mileage rate." This rate works for businesses, medical reasons, and in support of charitable organizations. For businesses, you can deduct 54.5 cents per mile for the miles you drive relating to business.

For example, if you drive 50 miles to meet a new client or pick up office supplies, you can deduct 54.5 cents per mile, totaling up to $27.5.

Anytime you go somewhere for business you need to record how many miles you traveled. Even if you only go one mile per day, it can add up for the entire year. Now, going from home to your office does not count, but any trip to a store, to a job, or other related business mileage can be counted.

Note: you can deduct vehicle mileage if you use your personal vehicle for business. It is imperative you record all mileage usage, including the personal details to show what is and is not related to business. Even if you do errands that are business and personal, make clear distinctions between each stop. If you are ever audited, you will need to show your documentation.

Meals Tax Deduction

There are reasons you may go out to eat and consider it a business expense. You might be dining with a client and talking business, trying to convince the person you are the right company to hire. You may be eating out to write a blog about the experience. As long as you discuss business during the meal or can consider the meal as part of a business necessity, you can deduct 50% of the meal and beverage costs. The idea is the meal has to fit the "ordinary and necessary" parameters.

Let's say you went on a run to pick up office supplies out of town because you live in a small town and it takes 30 miles to get to the office supply company. It took the entire day, so you needed food. You were working, therefore the meal counts.

If you dined out because you didn't want to go home for an hour and cook, before going back to the office, the meal would not count—unless—you discussed business with a partner, employee, or other person involved in the company.

Home-based Business Tax Deduction

If you run a business out of your home, you have tax deductions you can take. You do not want to miss these deductions at tax time, if you have enough to make it worthwhile. There is always a fine line between itemized deductions and standardized deductions that may be helpful or not. If you have minimal expenses with your business, then taking the itemized deductions is not worth it. You would pay out more in taxes than if you went with the standard deductions. You still file your home-based income, and TurboTax will add in any self-employed tax that needs to apply. However, you can deduct the home-office expenses as long as your home office. It is up to you to decide if the deductions are better being itemized or not.

First, you need to decide the percent of your home that your office takes up. For example, if your home office is 20% of the square footage of your home, you can deduct 20% of your bills for utilities, homeowner's insurance, HOA fees, security, repairs, maintenance, and other home related expenses like mortgage interest and property taxes.

Before you take the deduction or have your accountant take it, you need to understand the tax law.

You must use the office, only for business related work. It must be exclusive to your business- and business-related concepts. The office space must be separate from another area of the home. Now, you can use a divider, such as a room screen. The partition segments the office from home use areas. The amount of time you spend in your office is up to you, as long as each minute spent in the office area is for work only. For example, if you let your children into the office area and let them do their homework, you are no longer using the space "exclusively" for business and have violated the requirement. It means you cannot take the deductions.

Your family can come in and ask a question or you can take a personal phone call. The IRS says that as long as the interruptions are no more than would be at an actual commercial office building, they can occur.

Your home office has to be the office on file for the business and be the principal place you conduct your business. For employees who spend time at an office building part-time and work from home, they can still take the deduction as long as you are exclusive in the use of the office at home.

Note that if you have children and work from home, where your children are too young to be unsupervised, you can still take the deduction. You are considering part of the office as an in-workplace day care. Your office can also be used as storage, even if it is occasionally storing personal items. But your home must be the only place you work.

Calculating the home deduction is easier if you use the square footage. You should consider the square footage of your home and how much your office takes up. Let's say you have 250 square feet for your home, and your office is 8x8, which is 64 square feet. You would take 64 divided by 250 to gain the percentage. In this instance, the percentage is 25.6. You are allowed $5 per square feet, so 5 multiplied by 25.6 would give you the deduction amount, which is $128. These numbers are calculated using 2018 tax laws. It is imperative you check each year's tax laws to ensure nothing has changed about the home-based business deductions.

As mentioned above, you also have expenses you can deduct, such as utilities, property taxes, and more. It is important to learn the different options for these deductions.

A direct expense is one that is meant solely for the office, which means you deduct the entire amount. Long distance calls, painting the office, or a separate internet line for the office can all be a deduction.

Indirect expenses are those you will deduct based on percentage of office size. The electricity payment for the entire year is added up, and you can deduct the percentage of your office, meaning if 25.6 percent is your office space, you calculate the fees paid by 25.6 percent. Say you paid $400 for electricity, so 25.6 percent of that is the deducted amount or $102.

You can tell from the explanation that there are several opportunities to reduce the taxes owed by taking home-based business deductions. However, they can be complicated. Depending on the QuickBooks plan you might have TurboTax customer support to help you do your taxes. If you do not, it is something you can add with a TurboTax plan added to your QuickBooks plan.

The other choice is asking an accountant to review the information supplied and help you list all the deductions that apply. Thankfully, if you setup QuickBooks correctly for the type of business you have, its location, and you enter the bills you pay and reimbursements made for the deductions that count, it will be easier for you to ensure your accountant has everything they need to do your taxes correctly.

Remember, when we discussed adding bills and that you could reimburse yourself if you used a personal account for the purchase. Freelance and home-based businesses are where it truly matters that you do reimburse yourself for any personal payment for a business expense.

You could be missing deductions on your taxes because you are not an accountant or because you did not use an accounting software until now. Even if you are employed with a company and work from home, you might have missed some deductions in previous years. The good news is, you can usually make amendments and file for missed deductions. Again, it may take an accountant to go back through and do what needs to happen.

The above are the main deductions you do not want to forget. There are also some small business deductions to discuss.

Additional Deductions

- You can deduct expenses for cost of goods sold
- Capital expenses
- Some personal expenses

The cost of goods sold includes raw materials, freight, storage, cost of products, direct labor costs, and factory overhead. Note, the list includes additional deductions beyond what a freelance or self-employed worker at home would have.

Capital expenses include business start up costs, assets, and any improvements you make to your company.

When it comes to personal expenses, you have the option of making percentage deductions based on how frequently you use something for business versus personal. You get to divide the costs like the above discussion on utilities and your home office space.

If you are a freelancer, but you pay commissions, it is a deduction under the title "commissions." You need to record all commissions and show that the money was outgoing and was not straight income for you.

Companies that have employees may be able to deduct wagers and retirement plans. If you have a retirement plan because you set aside money on your own, it could be considered a business expense.

Any rental equipment or office rent is a deduction.

Interest paid, depending on the type of interest is still a deduction.

Taxes paid for assorted reasons may also be a deduction.

Insurance for the business, whether it is for the building, cars, or medical can be a deduction.

The above list is something you need to check on with the IRS each year. Tax laws change. Due to changes for small businesses, you may discover there are fewer deductions than in a previous year or if a new president vetoes laws, you might gain more deductions.

If you have any doubts or questions, seek an accountant to help you file your taxes. As a rule of thumb—keep all receipts whether you think something can be used as a deduction. You never know when you might need to provide the receipt as proof that you did or did not take deductions you were not supposed to.

CHAPTER 17

FILE MANAGEMENT SUGGESTIONS

Maintaining QuickBooks properly is not hard to do, if you keep up with the daily tasks. However, there are some things that are worth discussing to ensure you are using the various tasks and preventing issues later. For example, you need to backup your data, even if you use the online version.

Backing Up

You want to back up data anytime you use QuickBooks. Now, if you went into the program to look something up, it is not necessary to back up the information. However, if you went in and added a job, invoice, PO, created paychecks or anything else of importance—back it up.

1. Insert a disc, USB memory card, or other removable device into your computer.

2. Go to file.

3. Select "Copy File"

4. You have now backed everything up.

If you want to, you can back up your QuickBooks data online. You need a cloud storage account tied to QuickBooks. You can also link to QuickBooks storage options. There are usually fees for a business using online back up services. Check around to find the best cost for the options you obtain.

When you exit the program, it should ask you if you want to back up and how you wish to back up. There are prompts to follow for selecting the removable drive or backing up online. Simply follow the commands, name the file, and save.

Should any issues arise, you can get the data back.

- Get the back up files on the removable drive or go to your online source.
- Start QuickBooks and choose File
- Click "Open or Restore Company"
- Grab the file you want by clicking on it.
- Tell QuickBooks where to pull from and click next.
- You can then tell QuickBooks where you want the restore file to be saved.
- Save

When you restore QuickBooks because something occurred to the data, you are replacing the last file it thinks you had. As long as you are restoring the information, you have nothing to worry about. If you forgot to back it up and an issue occurred, you will need to input everything again.

You do not want to forget to back up because you never know what might happen. Furthermore, you want the file to be in a separate device or location because your computer could crash and lose everything.

You will back up each time you add new information to ensure you have the most recent file in your back up location.

Portable Files

You have the option of creating a portable file for use by other people like your accountant, or even taking home some of the work from your main location. Working with portable files means you use a copy.

1. Go to File

2. Create Copy

3. Select the portable company file

To open it, the person will choose file, open, and restore, and be able to look at the file after following some on screen instructions.

Accountant Files

Your accountant does not need the entire back up of your QuickBooks program. Intuit understands this, so they created an accountant's copy option. You will follow the back up procedure, but this time select Accountant's Copy. Your accountant can take the file, review it, make changes, and you can import the changes.

Obviously, there are many features in QuickBooks you may need to use or want to know how to use periodically as your business grows or you make changes to certain functions you perform. With backing up the data for other people like accountants, you have audit and closing year options, but those details are something a basic guide will not cover.

Going to training or watching training videos is one way to learn those methods if you need them. All this guide wants you to know—is—you have many options to help you with housekeeping functions should you need them, but for most users the additional choices are not imperative.

CHAPTER 18

FIXED ASSETS AND VEHICLE INFORMATION

Business ownership may include fixed assets and vehicles, which you need to record as part of your assets for business wealth and potential depreciation deductions. This section will assess the details you need to know about assets and vehicles to help you with potential deductions and showing your company's financial health.

Fixed Assets

Fixed assets are those that are typically "fixed" in place, such as a building or machinery bolted to a floor. For the purpose of QuickBooks, any asset you have like furniture, equipment and vehicles can be added to the fixed asset list.

The list will track the costs, depreciations, and other valuable information for accounting. You can also calculate and record depreciations for tax returns and financial statements. Lastly, the lists are helpful in calculating and recording gains and losses that occur from disposed fixed assets. As you may be aware, at tax time you will list information about your assets, such as disposing of a computer that no longer works.

Your accountant will already have a list of these items, if you have worked with someone consistently for years. However, it is always helpful to add these things into QuickBooks to ensure you are reaping the benefits and to make it easier on your accountant. The way to save money—make it easy—your accountant can use everything from QuickBooks, pull reports and import it into a tax filing system. It saves time.

Now that you understand what fixed assets are and why you want to have a comprehensive list, it is time to discuss fixed assets accounting.

Fixed Assets Accounting

This type of accounting helps you keep a list of the assets you have, records the depreciation, and records the disposal of any thing you had. From the list, you will be able to update the journal entries when you sell or dispose of assets.

The setup is simple:

1. Under Lists, choose Fixed Asset Item List

2. Add an item

3. Name the asset

4. Enter the description of the item, basically you are choosing an account to tie it to.

5. Describe the purchase information

6. Save the details

Later you might wish to update the fixed asset.

7. Go to lists, fixed asset item list
8. Open the item to edit
9. Update the information

You now have everything you need for recording your assets, whether it is a building, computer, or other asset your business has.

It is time to look at tracking vehicle mileage, as this can have an impact on asset calculations.

Vehicles as Assets

Whether you use a personal vehicle or have multiple vehicles for company use, you need to understand the older they are the less valuable they become. You want to have a vehicle list and a way to record the miles. It is two-fold. You will use the depreciation information on taxes, plus you can deduct mileage as discussed in a previous section.

1. Go to list

2. Select Customer and Vendor Profile

3. Vehicle List

4. Click New

5. Enter the Vehicle

6. Save the information.

We already discussed entering vehicle mileage per employee. You also need to enter the beginning mileage as part of the asset details.

Each time a trip is made, you will go into the vehicle mileage area, choose the vehicle, enter the date and time, the starting mileage, and ending mileage, and attribute it to a job if you need to, then save the trip details.

Since vehicle mileage rates may change each year, you also want to know how to update the information for tax time. In Enter Vehicle Mileage, there is a mileage rate option, where you can put in the current rates and save. You are able to go to the IRS website to find the updated mileage information each year.

You should check twice a year regarding the mileage rates because sometimes the IRS updates the information more than once.

CHAPTER 19

SALES TAX CHANGES AND INFORMATION

While this is a guide for QuickBooks, it is truly relevant to how you use the software to help you with accounting. In 2018, a law was passed based on a court case between certain states and giant retailers. Previous to the new law, companies did not have to charge sales tax on items shipped out of city. The new law states, if you mail items out of city, you must charge sales tax for the city and state where the item is going, and any other special taxes like county or jurisdiction.

There are new rules based on the state you ship to and they are not the same across the board. Some states who have adopted the law say if you ship $250,000 worth of items out of state into their state or 1,000 plus packages, you need to start charging sales tax.

The changes require you to spend more time on calculating sales tax for items shipped. There are handy websites that will help you figure out what you need to charge. These websites allow you to enter the address items are shipped to and will give you the tax code, plus the breakdown of the sales tax you will calculate.

The information you gain from the sales tax website can be entered on your invoices. Going back to the point of creating your invoices, you will enter tax information, such as whether the company is tax exempt or what tax you need to charge. Once you have the vendor information, you can keep it in QuickBooks to ensure you pull it up each time you create a new invoice.

Out of State Rules

Your local government page will help you find the new rules outlining whether the states you are shipping to have passed any sales tax law changes and adopted the new rules.

Looking by state, you will see what rules you need to follow.

It is important to keep track of the items you have shipped and the amount it totals to—you will want to prove why or why you did not collect tax—if you are audited.

Small businesses that rarely ship items out of their state are largely unconcerned with the tax law changes. Let's discuss the bookstore example. A person called the store, they saw a book when they visited over the summer and want to buy it. The book is $25.00, and shipping is $3.60. It is going to a state you did not ship to previously, therefore according to state rules, you don't have to charge taxes. But, let's say the next person is in Texas and you have shipped twenty items in the last six months to people in Texas. Now, you need to review the rules to see the amount set for charging tax. You may not qualify for the dollar amount, but how about the number of packages sent? It is an "or" situation, so if you send over $250,000 worth or you send 100 items, you may need to charge tax (this is an example and not reflecting any state).

In State Laws

If your state has adopted the sales tax law amendment, you are now responsible for charging sales tax to anyone you ship to in your state, regardless of the "out of state" rules. Some states are still ironing out the details. They may have a projected date for when you need to adopt the new rules, or you may need to be incompliance now. Check with your accountant and read the state rules.

There are two things you will want to do if you need to start charging sales tax when you ship in state.

1.   POS updates

2.   QuickBooks

If your point of sale system is part of QuickBooks, you can amend the sales tax information, as necessary. When you have QuickBooks for accounting purposes only, check to see if you can amend your sales tax to cover all parameters or if you need to manually enter the data when you make sales.

Many of the newer point of sales systems allow you to set up the most frequent sales taxes you are going to use to make it easier on you. You still use the online sales tax website to discover the code and the taxes to charge, but you get to keep it in the system to prevent yourself from working harder than you need to when you ship things.

For sales tax reports, make sure you are adding new sales tax information for each sales tax you charge. The reports are essential when it comes to filing your monthly sales tax payments.

Sales Tax Payments

In previous sections we discussed tax liabilities. Now we are going to go in-depth with the sales tax discussion.

Sales tax is collected each time you make a sale. You charge it using the POS system or when you create a receipt in QuickBooks. If you use QuickBooks, then you know the information is being saved and you can go into reports, create the sales tax report, and use that for your tax payments.

However, if you use two separate systems, you will need to update QuickBooks or use a different method for calculating the sales tax. Given that you have an option to record the monthly sales tax by reconciling your daily income split into the items purchased and tax collected, you will find it easy to create the report.

Even better, is sales tax payments are now made online. You are required to file the sales tax information and send the payment via electronic methods. If you do not pay your sales tax by the 15th of each month for the previous month, there is a hefty penalty. Do not let yourself get into a situation where you pay this horrible penalty. Due to the online system, you can import information from approved data sheets, such as sales tax reports created by QuickBooks.

By now, you should have a log in, unless you are opening a new business. Go to the state sales tax website, create a log in with username and password, and outline your company details.

If necessary, call your accountant to help you get this set up. During the setup phase, set up the payment method you are going to use, such as a direct electronic transfer from your bank account where the sales tax is deposited.

Using the month end reports, calculate the deposit information sans the sales tax paid. Any paid outs; mailed out of city and out of state information, and other information requested by the tax website should be entered. The online document will calculate what you owe, and you can follow the steps to make a payment.

Since the tutorial is about QuickBooks, the details on filing Sales Tax are not complete. They are straightforward, and your state is on hand if you have questions. Once the payments are made record them in QuickBooks as an expense, so you can reconcile your account correctly for the ACH payment that came out of your bank account.

CHAPTER 20

QUICKBOOKS TIPS

You have made it this far in the QuickBooks guide. Should you have a handle on most QuickBooks functions, but want some quick tips—this is the place to be reading.

Work Flow Tips for Bookkeeping

To make life easier as the bookkeeper for a business, there are tasks you should keep on top of based on your job description. People who come in once a week to work as a bookkeeper may not find all the details here, helpful. But if you are an in-house bookkeeper consider the suggestions.

- Daily – enter money in and out transactions.
- Daily – send estimates and sales forms to clients
- Daily – enter new assets and liabilities
- Daily – check incoming bank transactions
- Weekly – look for unpaid invoices and bills (accounts receivable and payable)
- Weekly – add and edit any new vendor and customer details

- Weekly – add and edit services and product information
- Weekly – monitor the bank information
- Monthly – reconcile your bank accounts
- Monthly – run profit and loss statements from the previous month
- Review any problems
- Quarterly – check in with your accountant and create the accountant report

These task tips help you keep on top of the tasks, so the jobs are easier. What could take an hour may only take a few minutes each due to the upkeep you have. There are also fewer potential mistakes when you are entering on a daily, weekly, or monthly basis regarding the tasks.

The above is also a suggested timetable that may not fit your business model or job description. You have to decide what works for you and your company.

Freelancers may have fewer updates on a daily basis due to closed service orders and payments made. As an example, a person may be paid once a month for an entire months' work, which is where tracking the jobs is important and ensuring the freelancer invoices for all work before the monthly cut off date.

Designing your Business Model

QuickBooks is wonderful because it has numerous features for various business models. Yet, you still need to incorporate as much information as possible to design the business model and make QuickBooks as useful as it can possibly be.

Freelancers and home-based self-employed individuals may benefit from the freelance version or the next step up, but the way to benefit is to ensure you create a business model and schedule of tasks for what you do and the time frame it happens in. A good rule is to enter as much information as possible into QuickBooks and ignore what you find is not essential.

Custom Fields

QuickBooks is designed on the premise that your small business will have similar classes or categories for items based on tax details. Accountants need specific information for deductions and income allocations. Creating custom fields may be unnecessary or may not help you.

On tax forms, there are places for "other" income or expenses. You are required to be specific in your description when you use the "other" category. You can also create your own, so you show the specific business income or expenses that do not fit in the generalized tax categories.

Should you find it necessary to create custom fields, you are more apt to see a drop-down list to help you. However, you can also add "other" and customize something special. Whether you need it for taxes, or it is something to help you see a difference in a QuickBooks report, at least you do have the option of adding custom fields.

You do so by going into the area that is suited to the custom creation, such as Vendor, class, and adding a new category type.

User Roles and Permissions

There are times when you want admin, for administrator, where you are able to perform all functions in QuickBooks, such as when you are the only user. For companies who have multiple employees using the timesheet functions, you will want to create user roles and permissions.

Under Company, go to Users, Set up users, and Roles.

- Look at the roles list tab to see if there is a role that fits your employee.
- Create a role if necessary.
- Click edit to add more functionality or take permissions away.
- Save the changes made.

Now, you have a way for other users to access what they need to do, without being able to view confidential business documents. As you are aware, QuickBooks is designed to work with a certain number of users and may function as the service or sales software for your company. You want permissions restricted for the level your employee is, while retaining higher permissions for those of increased status in the company.

Transaction History

QuickBooks helps you maintain information and sometimes you might have trouble finding specific transactions, but for one reason or another you need to review the details. You can do so, by going into reports, selecting transaction history, and filling out the prompts it provides. It will help you find a transaction, even if it has been a year or more since you made the sale.

Linking Email

Another helpful feature of QuickBooks is linking with various accounts, including your email. Many vendors and clients use email to avoid paper waste. You will find you are sending out emails with invoices versus faxes, calling, or seeing a vendor in person. Linking your email is helpful because you can send the invoice, reminders, and credit memos directly to the company via email. QuickBooks will link with Outlook, Yahoo, Gmail, and other email operators. You do not have to import your contacts, you just tell QuickBooks you want to email something, and you will go to the email to attach the invoice through QuickBooks.

CONCLUSION

Congratulations you have reached the end of the guide. You have this guide at your disposal for whenever you have questions, forget how to do a task, or need to learn something you glossed over in the previous study.

Use this guide as a means of helping you learn QuickBooks, as well as feeling confident that it's the right decision to add it to your company. It's understandable that you might have begun work as a freelancer and your company took off, so now you need bookkeeping and accounting software. You may have bought an older business and want to upgrade its capabilities. No matter what situation you are in, you have the option of bringing in QuickBooks as a new or existing company.

If you are ever unsure of how to launch the program, contact QuickBooks or have your accountant stop by for the installation. Established companies will have more of a transition than someone starting a new business. It might require more time and help.

You also have training classes and self-paced learning experience to help you become an expert on the functionality of QuickBooks.

When you start using QuickBooks, it is best to use every option it has that applies to your company. You do not want to start using a portion of the software now and then try to add more functions later. For example, you might set up the bare minimum for writing employee checks, but later you want to use the full functionality. Going backwards is more difficult than if you set it up right the first time.

Thank you for purchasing this guide and hopefully you have found it helpful to your business needs.

CPSIA information can be obtained
at www.ICGtesting.com
Printed in the USA
BVHW091134020919
557352BV00016B/706/P

9 781733 370530